W9-CEI-931

Pause for Thought

Making Time for Prayer, Jesus, and God

Gerald O'Collins, SJ

Paulist Press
New York / Mahwah, NJ

Scripture quotations contained herein are either from the author's own translations from the original Greek, or are from the New Revised Standard Version: Catholic Edition Copyright © 1989 and 1993, by the Division of Christian Education of the National Council of the Churches of Christ in the United States of America. Used by permission. All rights reserved.

Cover and book design by Lynn Else

Copyright © 2011 by Gerald O'Collins, SJ

All rights reserved. No part of this book may be reproduced or transmitted in any form or by any means, electronic or mechanical, including photocopying, recording, or by any information storage and retrieval system without permission in writing from the Publisher.

Library of Congress Cataloging-in-Publication Data

O'Collins, Gerald.
    Pause for thought : making time for prayer, Jesus, and God / Gerald O'Collins.
        p. cm.
    Includes index.
    ISBN 978-0-8091-4710-6 (alk. paper)
    1. Jesus Christ—Biblical teaching. 2. Prayer—Biblical teaching. 3. God (Christianity)—Biblical teaching. 4. Catholic Church—Doctrines. I. Title.
    BT203.O36 2011
    232'.8—dc22

                                                                    2011000906

Published by Paulist Press
997 Macarthur Boulevard
Mahwah, New Jersey 07430

www.paulistpress.com

Printed and bound in the
United States of America

Contents

CONTENTS

Contents

Preface

This book is designed for those who face full programs at home and at work but still want to pause regularly to reflect upon the deeper realities of life. Even if their daily diaries allow only a few minutes for quietly pondering the real agenda of human existence, they know that prayerfully thinking of Jesus and God will bring into focus the things that really matter. Without such a frequent pause for thought, their lives will lack spiritual depth.

This book groups the chapters into five parts:

1. Prayer
2. The Coming and Mission of Jesus
3. The Suffering and Death of Jesus
4. The Resurrection of Jesus and his Risen Life
5. Our God

Each chapter stands by itself and does not presuppose what comes before or follows. Readers can pick and choose, taking up the chapters in the order they wish. Some chapters are quite short, others much longer. That difference may suit some readers, who on given days have less or more time for this book.

However they tackle what I have written, I will be more than grateful if this book helps readers to engage each day in some brief, spiritual reflection and prayer.

Earlier versions of some of the material contained in this book have appeared in *The Pastoral Review* and *The Tablet*, and are reprinted with permission. For biblical quotations I generally follow the New Revised Standard Version, but, on occasions, I translate directly from the Greek text of the New Testament.

With much affection I dedicate this book to John and Monica Ellison, whose love and hospitality have supported my life for decades.

Part One

PRAYER

1
Six Images of Prayer

How can we settle down quietly into prayer? What images might help us engage more easily in prayer and do so on a regular basis? Let me suggest six images that might let us quietly settle into prayer.

Prayer as Going into Deep Silence

Prayer means letting ourselves go into deep silence in the presence of God. Here one of my favorite comparisons comes from those who have an enthusiasm for bird-watching. Over the years I have enjoyed the friendship of two men, one a journalist and the other an academic, who were both dedicated bird-watchers. They thought nothing of rising in the early hours of the morning and heading out into the countryside to conceal themselves in a swampy field or up to their waists in a pond. They endured the cold and put up with cramps in their legs, as they spent hours intently looking through their field glasses. They knew that they needed to keep very still and quiet—all eyes and ears, one might say. When light gradually came into the sky, they would hear and catch sight of many birds and perhaps even spot some species they had never seen before. They treasured bird-watching so much that they found it very worthwhile to spend hours of their time concealing themselves in marshes and putting up with considerable discomfort for hours on end.

Prayer involves letting ourselves become all eyes and ears, as we wait very quietly for light to dawn and God to come through to us. In prayer we become all eyes and ears, because we want to be helped to see something of God and hear some word from God, perhaps even something surprisingly new and unexpected. Being very still and very quiet like a dedicated bird-watcher pictures one characteristic posture for prayer.

One might vary the image by turning from the habits of bird-watchers to the peace and silence that every now and then we experience in two people who have enjoyed years of loving friendship, especially two older people who have spent many years together as husband and wife. Such a devoted, elderly couple may say or do very little, and are simply happy to stay for hours in each other's company—silently present to one another.

Whatever way we want to fill out the image, prayer should help us to be peacefully "there" in God's company. Prayer leads us to spend our time silently attentive to the presence of the One who loves us so much and wants to communicate light and life to us.

Prayer as Looking

Gazing steadfastly at something or someone is a second, related image of how prayer can take place. When we are out-of-doors enjoying a visit to a lovely forest or garden, we might allow ourselves to look at some particular tree, shrub, or bush of vivid roses. This is a well tried method for focusing our spiritual feelings and thoughts so that they too will grow and flower. From created beauty and life we can lift our gaze gently to the uncreated beauty and life of God.

When they remain indoors in a church, chapel, or room for prayer, many people let their gaze rest on an icon, a crucifix, a flickering sanctuary lamp, a statue, a picture, or the tabernacle where the Blessed Sacrament is reserved. Such peaceful, steady looking lets prayer emerge and flourish.

The image of prayer as steady looking can appeal to the example of John's Gospel. It opens by announcing that "the Word became flesh and dwelt amongst us, and *we contemplated* his glory" (1:14). This Gospel forms one long contemplative gazing at the incarnate Son of God that reaches a climax when Thomas looks at the risen One and declares: "My Lord, and my God" (20:28). Contemplation by the community ("we") at the beginning and by an individual (Thomas) at the end brackets the whole story, and invites attentive readers in their turn to gaze in prayer at the incarnate and risen Christ.

Such contemplative looking at Jesus feeds off the titles that recur in the pages of this Gospel. Gazing at Jesus, we can simply and quietly say: "You are the Light of the world. You are the Lamb of God. You are the Bread of Life. You are the Resurrection and the Life. You are the Way, the Truth and the Life. You are my Lord and my God."

We might even imagine how certain persons pictured in John's Gospel as being very close to him gazed steadily at Jesus during his lifetime. We could join the beloved disciple in looking with love at Jesus. Or we could gaze at him with the eyes of that family of Bethany to whom he was bound by deep love: Martha, Mary, and their brother Lazarus. We might even think of joining the Mother of Jesus when she looked at him during the marriage feast at Cana or during the hours that he hung dying on the cross.

If it seems presumptuous and even daunting to join close friends of Jesus in looking at him, we might turn to an anonymous group of Gentiles who had arrived in Jerusalem to worship at the Passover festival. They approach Philip and say to him: "Sir, we would like to see Jesus" (John 12:20–21). Their request readily turns into our prayer: "Jesus, I want to see you.

I want to see you today and all the days of my life. I want to see you and come to you with faith. I want to look at you with steadfast love and lasting devotion."

Prayer as Talking to God and Ourselves

Over the centuries prayer has often been described as being a heart-to-heart conversation with the God whom we love. We may carry on that conversation in our own words or in words that come from the psalms: "Protect me, O God, for in you I take refuge. O Lord, you are my rock, my fortress, my deliverer. O Lord, how great you are. How great is your name in all the earth. O God, be gracious to me, and heal me."

Or else our talking in prayer may take the form of talking to Jesus himself. Many people take up and repeat as a kind of mantra a prayer that early Christians used in Aramaic and Greek: "*Maranatha*: come, Lord Jesus" (1 Cor 16: 22; Rev 22: 20). The "Jesus Prayer" practiced by Eastern Christians also involves a heart-to-heart speaking to Jesus. They repeat over and over again: "Jesus, Son of David, have mercy on me." Or, more briefly, "Jesus, have mercy on me."

Here all kinds of variations come into use: "Jesus, my love, have mercy on me. Jesus, you are my love." A traditional refrain ran: "Jesus is Lord; Jesus is King; Jesus is our everything." We can make these words deeply personal: "Jesus, you are my Lord; Jesus, you are my King; Jesus, you are my everything."

Such heart-to-heart conversation can well include talking gently to ourselves, like a mother talking to a restless, depressed child. This is a practice as old as the psalms. So often the psalmists speak to themselves: "Praise the Lord, my soul." Or else they question themselves: "O my soul, why are you downcast?"

Prayer as Depth Experience

Prayer involves deeply experiencing God and ourselves. Without prayer we will never truly know ourselves and know God. Through praying we dive deep to discover the hidden depths of God but also the hidden depths of ourselves—what 1 Peter 3:4 calls "the hidden person of the heart." Prayer takes us down into the heart of things, the deepest center of our existence. It lets distracting things drop away, purifying us and making us grow in understanding ourselves and God.

We might picture this depth experience as starting on the surface of bubbling, seething mudflats. Prayer takes us below all that dirt and confusion, right down to deep springs of water below. At that depth everything is quietly flowing and crystal clear.

St. Augustine classically expressed this image of prayer: "Lord, that I might know myself, that I might know thee!" As we might say, "Lord that I might go down into the depths of myself, that I might go down into the hidden depths of your life and your love."

Prayer as Putting Our Heads into Our Hearts

Occasionally people admit: "When I try to pray, nothing happens. My mind goes blank." But, more often, the problem is that too much happens. Too many ideas flood into our heads. Or, to vary the image, our minds go racing off in all directions. Or, even more frequently, too many feelings flood into our minds and fill our heads with babble.

When we try to pray, all kinds of fears and worries can overwhelm us. Seemingly they rob us of our freedom to pray and even leave us feeling paralyzed. Or else we may find ourselves slipping away into daydreams about something to which we are attached and which we very much want to have and hang onto.

At other times what gets in the way of prayer are all kinds of resentments that boil up. Instead of praying, we find ourselves fighting old battles over and over again in our heads. Our mind can be filled with angry voices. Instead of praying, we hear ourselves shouting at others in our heads.

Years ago, when I was on retreat and already several days into silence and prayer, a group from Alcoholics Anonymous arrived at the same retreat house for a two-day spiritual course. Everywhere around the building the management put urns of coffee for them, and from six in the morning through to midnight they consumed prodigious amounts of coffee. These members of AA themselves pinned up on the board various key sayings from those who had created their organization. The one that struck me most declared: "Resentment is the number one killer. It's a luxury we cannot afford."

Yes, resentment is a luxury none of us can afford. In particular, it can prove a number one killer in our life of prayer. It takes over what happens in our heads and stops us facing and finding God in our hearts.

In such situations a very simple response may be best. We can quietly breathe in and out, as we say "Jesus." His holy name can banish the inner demons of resentment. No matter how much we feel ourselves to be under attack from angry thoughts, Jesus is there to calm our heads and take us peacefully into our hearts. His name can always work its magic and put our busy heads into the peace of our hearts.

Prayer as Being Delivered from False Images

Life-giving prayer can take place only between the real God and the real self. Prayer delivers us from false images of ourselves and false images of God. This is a sixth and last way of viewing prayer.

God wants to save the real "me," not some imaginary or false "me" that I might present in prayer. We need to bring our real selves to prayer, those selves that experience all the deep joys, sharp pains, and nagging worries that make up the actual situation of our daily lives.

Facing our real selves involves dropping false images of God, a God whom we would prefer to make in our image and likeness. All too easily we can create for ourselves a false image of God as severe, demanding, and out to "get us," or else an image of God as softly "liberal" and ready to accommodate conveniently any of our whims. Prayer should open us up to God as God is, the God who may wish to upset our values and lead us in ways that we would prefer not to go.

We can make idols of our career, our beauty, our health, and our status in society. We can also do worse and fashion false images of God. Genuine prayer means facing the real "me" in the presence of the real God, as the tax collector did (Luke 18:9–14). Unlike the Pharisee in that parable, the sinful tax collector presented his real person, face to face with the real God.

Such then are six images of prayer: as going into deep silence, as steady looking, as talking to God and ourselves, as depth experience, as putting our heads into our hearts, and as being delivered from false images. Our preferred image of prayer may be one of these six, or we may find that the image we experience may vary from one of these images to another. What matters is that we do pray—regularly and fruitfully every day of our life. If my account of these images helps any readers to settle down in such prayer, I will be more than grateful.

2

Prayer as Being Questioned

In films, in novels and, for that matter, in real life, the first words we hear from someone can be tremendously important, even decisive. In works of fiction, someone's first words can give us an excellent clue as to what that character is like and what he or she is going to do. In real life, the first words we hear from someone may create a lasting friendship, even from the very start.

When we read the four Gospels, it is fascinating to notice the first words coming from Jesus himself. In the Gospel of John, for example, the opening words from Jesus take the form of a question. Andrew and a friend are struck by what John the Baptist says about Jesus ("Look, here is the Lamb of God!") and start walking along behind Jesus. He turns around, sees them following, and asks: "What are you looking for?" (John 1:36–38).

At one level the question Jesus puts is straightforward: "What are you after? What is your purpose in trailing along after me?" But his question hints at a possible, deeper meaning: "What are you looking for in life?" Without forcing himself on the two men, Jesus confronts and gently challenges their most fundamental aspirations and intentions. It is an extraordinary way of initiating Andrew and his companion for what is going to become a deep and lifelong relationship with Jesus.

Jesus calls the two men into question, just as he will call us into question whenever we spend time with him in prayer. A heart-to-heart conversation with Jesus will, sooner or later, bring up the questions: What am I looking for? What have I set my heart on? What do I finally hope to find and to do with my life?

In John's Gospel Jesus continues to ask many deep and even disturbing questions. A prayerful reading of that Gospel invites us to stop at the questions of Jesus and really let them sink in. If we do that, we will find in prayer the word Jesus addresses to us taking the shape of searching questions.

At the end of chapter 6 of John, many people are giving up on Jesus, and he says a little sadly to the core group of his disciples: "Will you also go away?" (6:67). Now, there is more than one way of our leaving Jesus, just as there are many ways of not staying with him fully. We can stay with Jesus in a halfhearted way that is not truly living his life. We have not gone away from him, yet we do not fully belong to him. We remain near him rather than *with* him. We need a lot of honesty in our prayer if we are to take time over that question from Jesus: "Will you also go away?"

There are many other questions asked by Jesus in the Gospel of John. We could spend a lifetime hearing them and praying over them—right through to that awesomely direct question Jesus puts three times to Peter in the last chapter: "Do you love me?" (21:15–17). Jesus does not ask Peter: "Have you a good plan for organizing the missionary campaign of the Church? Do you think that you have the qualities to lead that campaign successfully?" Instead, loving friendship is all that Jesus wants from Peter or from any of us.

All the questions Jesus puts to us in prayer and in life finally come down to that one, searching question: "Do you love me?" At the end, he questions us only about our love. Please, dear readers, give that love a chance by letting Jesus put that question to you in your prayer.

3

The Case Against Prayer

One can construct an impressive case against prayer, or at least against personal prayer practiced outside the context of community worship. Would we not be better advised giving our spare time directly to others? Surely we are reaching out to God and in real contact with God when we work generously for others?

In his picture of the Last Judgment, Jesus called on his followers to show hospitality toward strangers, to feed the hungry, and in other ways to help those who are in distress and need our help. Jesus did *not* say: "I was hungry and you prayed for me. I was a stranger and you added my name to your list of petitions at the end of your morning period of mental prayer." Jesus wanted his disciples to be involved with those who are in desperate need and who rely on us to come to their assistance. Surely if we are involved with such people, we are involved with God?

As a popular hymn expects, "They shall know that we are Christians by our love." This refrain does not claim, "They shall know that we are Christians by our prayer." In any case some people who pray and maybe pray a good deal may seem less than attractive and sometimes even downright disagreeable persons. What good has prayer done to them? And, for that matter, what good does prayer do to us?

When filling out our case against prayer, we might also claim that there is a certain sense of unreality when we lay down for ourselves a daily schedule for prayer. Praying at fixed times and in fixed places runs counter to the natural rhythms and spontaneity of life. We don't prescribe a heart-to-heart conversation with someone every morning at 6.30. We arrange business interviews and working breakfasts on that basis. But prayer is meant to be a heart-to-heart conversation with God, not a business interview. Can we "legislate" conditions and terms for prayer?

Prayer as Indispensable

And yet a case against prayer will not rouse too much enthusiasm among the followers of Jesus. Prayer is not an accessory, not even a valuable accessory, to Christian life—something added on to make a better Christian out of a good one. Right from the New Testament times, a follower of Jesus has been understood to be someone who gives regular time to prayer. The very first Christian letter that has survived insists: "...pray continually. Give thanks whatever happens; for this is what God wills for you in Christ Jesus" (1 Thess 5:17–18).

The *Didache*, probably written about AD 90 and so the oldest Christian document outside the New Testament, enjoined the regular practice of daily prayer, along with generous help toward those in need.

From the very beginning of the Church's history, the life of the baptized has always disclosed two basic signs that characterize the community they enter. Their new orientation toward God expresses itself in the practice of worship and prayer (a vertical sign) and in loving service toward other human beings (a horizontal sign). To the extent that either the vertical or the horizontal sign is missing in the life of Christians, their discipleship remains retarded.

In particular, the neglect of prayer will bring a "power failure" in the life of faith and love. Over the long haul and even over the short haul, a faith that shows itself in love (Gal 5:7) will not persevere when prayer is persistently neglected. We will no longer view the situation around us with the eyes of love if failure in prayer has let the light of faith grow dim or even go out.

This is not to say that praying is or will always be easy. But the fact that something is difficult does not mean that it is not worth doing. It is hardly a twenty-first-century discovery that prayer can be difficult. Giving oneself consistently to prayer can be an heroic and even agonizing struggle (Rom 15:30; Col 4:12). On the one occasion when Mark's Gospel describes Jesus at prayer, he was overwhelmed with such horror and anguish that the Christian tradition named the episode "the agony in the garden" (Mark 14:32–36).

All Is Gift

Among the other blessings that it brings, regular prayer reminds us that Christianity is not a "do-it-yourself" religion. The divine grace is the one and only thing that really matters. The gifts of God, and not mere human achievements, make our lives successful. As St. Augustine of Hippo insisted, when God crowns our merits, he does nothing else but crown his gifts.

Setting aside regular times for daily prayer may cut into busy, even overburdened, timetables. But having such fixed times recalls the basic truth of our existence: we are always openhanded before God—as those who receive everything and own nothing. Daily prayer will encourage us to be full of wonder and radically grateful for all that the infinitely loving God does for us and gives us day by day.

Georges Bernanos closed his classic *Diary of a Country Curate* with the words of a young priest who is dying of cancer: "All is gift." In a 1972 conference for the alumni of "Guest House," a center that cares for alcoholic priests, religious, and bishops, Father Philip Donnelly ended a remarkable address with these words: "We can sum up everything by saying that what we have learned at Guest House is this: that in all of our limitations, in all of our imperfections and sinfulness and sins, we have learned what I hope is the undying lesson for each of us...that only in Christ are we great." Prayer will keep alive that conviction: it is through the crucified and risen Jesus that God offers all of us the true gift of greatness.

Results of Prayer

What impact does prayer have on believers, collectively and individually? I have long cherished two answers that came to me in the 1970s. First, in an article for *Commonweal* on the new order of Mass and the future of the liturgy (March 27, 1970), Father Gerard Sloyan may have shown himself unduly pessimistic and even depressed. But his opening statement compelled assent: "Unless the general quality of liturgical celebration improves, nothing noteworthy can be hoped for. Ultimately it is not a question of whether liturgies shall be fixed or fluid, but of the *prayerful character* which underlies them or is absent from them" (italics mine). How else will those who preside and those who participate in liturgy grow in such a "prayerful character" except through the regular practice of personal prayer? Without their being personally changed by their daily program of time spent with the Lord, those who lead and share in any liturgy will not be able to develop any liturgical celebrations with a truly prayerful character. As a classic Latin adage puts it, "No one gives what he or she doesn't have (*nemo dat quod non habet*)."

The second answer about the impact of prayer turned up a few years later in Rome. A friend, who had spent a good deal of time in Italy working on her doctoral dissertation before becoming a professor of fine arts in Australia, returned to Rome on a working visit. "Have you noticed anything different since you were here last time?" I asked her. "Well, yes, someone has changed profoundly," she told me. "In the pension where I stayed several years ago there was a girl who seemed quite lost. This time round I found her to be so much happier and didn't know why until I knocked on her door one morning. She was sitting there with the Gospels open in front of her."

That experience made me think of one or two friends who had assured me: "Some of those who pray are less than attractive, even downright disagreeable." I wanted to go back to these friends and ask: "Can you really show me some cases of men or women who pray regularly and remain unhappy or even cantankerous?"

The Practice of Prayer

With prayer it is the practice, not the theory, that counts. There was a point to a complaint I read in May 1969: "Very often more time is spent talking about prayer than in praying. As is the case of so many other religious values, discussion of the value has become a substitute for the value itself" (J. R. Sheets, *Review for Religious*). That same month another writer put the same point more succinctly: "Prayer is more a matter of practice and less a subject for theorizing than any other subject conceivable" (*Herder Correspondence*).

As a value and a practice, prayer is indispensable. Nowhere do we read in either the Old or the New Testament that someone was prompted by God to invent prayer. Prophets, Jesus himself, and some of the leaders in the emerging Church introduced new things that shape forever our relationship with God. The institution of the Eucharist at the Last Supper offers a spectacular example of such religious "inventions" or "additions." Prayer, however, is not like that. In both the Old and

New Testament it is simply taken for granted that human beings pray and should pray. The indispensable value of prayer was understood to justify itself in practice.

Three Recommendations

Let me conclude by making three recommendations. First, we need some definite timetable for our daily prayer. Unless we fix some place and time for prayer, we won't pray regularly.

Second, we need some method of approach to prayer if it not going to lapse into aimless mental wanderings. That is not to say that we should stick rigidly to some way of praying, year in and year out. In and through prayer God will undoubtedly draw us to change the type and method of prayer we adopt. Yet, at whatever stage we find ourselves, we need some method of approach for the time and place we have set for prayer.

Third, in the *Soul of the Apostolate* Jean-Baptiste Chautard compares physical work, study, and prayer. Physical work, he argues, can be hard, but study is harder, and prayer the hardest of all. This may not be the best of comparisons. Prayer, Teresa of Avila, declared, consists not in thinking much but in loving much. During a time of consolation, that "loving much" can prove delightful, even a time of extraordinary joy.

Nevertheless, a strange kind of hardiness can envelop our praying and our desire to hold ourselves steadily in the presence of God. At those moments we might remember something proposed by Jean-Nicholas Grou: it is the image of ourselves, waiting quietly like a little, grey donkey for God to help us.

4
Two Texts for Prayer

After chapters dedicated more to the "theory" of prayer, it may be good to complete part one of this book by reflecting on particular texts that can feed into prayer. Let me take up now two biblical texts: one from St. Luke and the other from the Book of Revelation. The next chapter will show how two poetical texts might also feed into prayer.

The Sending of the Seventy-two

The Gospel of Luke is full of treasures, marvelous passages that are found only in that Gospel and that have shaped Christian life, prayer, and imagination from the beginning. Down through the ages, the parables of the Good Samaritan (10:29–37) and the rich man and Lazarus (16:19–31) have challenged believers to come to the aid of the impoverished and distressed people they meet. Christian prayer has taken up the wonderful prayers with which Luke opens his story of Jesus: the *Magnificat* from the Virgin Mary (1:46–55), the *Benedictus* from Zechariah (1:68–79) and the *Nunc Dimittis* from Simeon (2:29–32). Artists have returned again and again to the scenes of the Annunciation (1:26–38) and the Nativity (2:1–20).

Another treasure comes in Luke's account of Jesus sending seventy-two disciples on a mission to announce the kingdom of God (10:1–20). What is so special about this story? It turns up in the Gospel shortly after an episode that seems much more important: the sending on mission of the Twelve 9:1–6). And yet the sending of the seventy-two is a story with which each of us can and should identify in prayer and life.

Like Matthew and Mark, Luke reports how Jesus called by name Peter, James, and John and other founding fathers of the Church and sent them on a trial mission during his ministry. These twelve were a unique group: they followed Jesus during his lifetime and became official witnesses to his resurrection from the dead. They were already *the* leaders of the small Christian community when the Holy Spirit came at the first Pentecost. Empowered then by the Spirit, the twelve launched the spread of the Church.

These twelve apostles stand there as gigantic figures at the start of Christianity. It is not always easy for us later Christians to identify with them. In some ways they seem, larger than life, like the large stained-glass windows that display them in some churches or the huge statues of them that line the cathedral of Rome, the Basilica of St. John Lateran.

Unlike the twelve apostles, the much larger group of seventy-two disciples sent out by Jesus during his ministry seems much closer to us. They went on mission in pairs, two by two. We do not know their names and what happened to them later after the resurrection of Jesus and the outpouring of the Holy Spirit. Were they all men? Probably not. A few chapters earlier Luke has mentioned such women as Mary Magdalene, Joanna, and Susanna (Luke 8:1–3), who were close disciples of Jesus and traveled with him during his ministry. The seventy-two sent on mission could well have included some of these female disciples, maybe some married couples. We do not know this for sure, but we certainly cannot exclude the possibility.

What we do learn from Luke's Gospel is that Jesus gave a larger group of his followers, seventy-two of them, a missionary vocation. What happened to them later? Were some of them or even all of them among the 120 gathered to pray in Jerusalem with Mary the mother of Jesus, Peter, and the rest of the apostles before the coming of the Holy Spirit (Acts 1:12–15)? Presumably some of the seventy-two became leaders in the Christian Church after Pentecost. We do not know the particulars.

What we know from Luke is that Jesus also gave a missionary task to a much wider group than the twelve. In prayer we can easily identify imaginatively with that larger group, rank-and-file disciples of the Lord, to whom he gave a triple task: to bring peace wherever they went, to heal the sick, and to preach the kingdom of God.

That commission of the seventy-two disciples belongs to every baptized Christian. We are all to be people of peace, men and women who bring others the peace of Christ wherever we go. We too are called to serve others: to heal the sick, to feed the hungry, to visit the lonely, and to encourage the desperate. We too are called to proclaim the kingdom of God and tell people of the wonderful and powerful new life that Jesus has brought into the world. The story of the sending of the seventy-two vividly reminds us of what we all should do as missionaries for Christ. We can turn this story into a prayer of self-examination. Do I bring others the peace of the Lord wherever I go? Do I care for the sick and the needy? Do I spread the word about the blessings that have come through the person and presence of Jesus Christ?

The New Jerusalem

It could be interesting to run a survey and ask people what their favorite city is. The city they like best might be Paris, London, or Amsterdam. Or it might be Boston, New York, Chicago, or San Francisco. Others might name a city in Africa, Asia, or Latin America. Some might name Rome, Florence, or Venice. Most of us seem to have our favorite city.

Yet we would probably have to admit that there was something wrong with our chosen city. Perhaps it is situated on the banks of a river that is badly polluted. Or perhaps our favorite city lacks sufficient parks and gardens. Or maybe it is run by a corrupt city administration. Or perhaps it suffers from a high crime rate and the streets are not well lit. Whatever the problems are, no favorite city is perfect. There are always some drawbacks.

A passage from the Book of Revelation 22:1–7 invites us to imagine a favorite city with no problems and no drawbacks. A crystal clear stream, the river of life, runs down the middle of the main street. Gardens line the banks of the river, with a tree of life on either bank busily bearing crops of fruit each month of the year. There are no problems with city administration and public security. Everything is in the hands of God the Father and his Son, Jesus Christ. Crime does not exist, because the city is full of God's servants who joyfully worship their divine Lord. There are no problems with the city lighting because it is always daytime and the sunlight of God streams down on the inhabitants.

This is the imaginative way in which the author of Revelation pictures his favorite city, the new Jerusalem, the city to which we are called home.

In prayer and at other times, we can find ourselves asking, perhaps a little anxiously: What will the future bring me? How will it unfold? Ultimately our future is nothing fearful but something full of life. The Lord is calling us home to a new city, his favorite city, the new Jerusalem. He is coming to bring us home to that marvelous city of the future. We can look forward and with great joy make our own the prayer with which the Book of Revelation and the whole Bible ends: "Come, Lord Jesus."

5

Two Poems of the Passion

Two anonymous poems (from the late thirteenth and the fourteenth century, respectively), the one subtle and laconic and the other splendidly direct, can set the mood for our contemplating the passion of Jesus.

In the earlier poem the speaker is a Christian who suffers with Mary as she keeps her lonely vigil at the foot of the cross.

> Now goeth sun under wood—Me rueth, Mary, thy faire
>   rode [face].
> Now goeth sun under tree—Me rueth, Mary, thy Son and
>   thee.

Sunset on Good Friday provides the setting for this poem. The picture is drawn with economy and established in two stages. The sun is going down behind a/the "wood," which is then identified as the tree on which hangs the crucified Jesus. By repeating "Now" the poem evokes the moment when light drains out of the sky. We may shrink from seeing the light of day go, but we are powerless before a sunset. The passage of the sun suggests the dying and irreversible death of Jesus. Both his death and the onset of darkness seem inexorable.

Using a pun on "sun" (twice) and "Son" (once), the speaker grieves ("me rueth") for the suffering of Mary and her Son. The repetition of "Me rueth" underlines the deep compassion felt by the speaker. As the sun goes down, he sees Mary's lovely face ("thy faire rode") lit up by the light of the setting sun. He is moved by the pain on her fair face, and grieves for this lovely lady and her dead Son.

This taut poem also appears to link the descent of the sun with the descent of Christ from the cross. The sun sinks below the horizon, just as Christ will sink from the cross into the arms of his Mother at the foot of his cross.

In July 2008 a highlight of World Youth Day in Sydney, Australia, came for many people with the Stations of the Cross that took them through the city to the crucifixion scene on the shore of the harbor. On television millions followed that reenactment of the first Good Friday. Later many more saw those Stations on DVD and heard the music, readings, and meditations that made them so religiously powerful.

In that presentation of the Stations of the Cross, the sun set just as Christ died and the chill of a winter's evening arrived. He was taken down from the cross, with darkness spreading across the gentle waves of Sydney harbor. The climax of those Stations of the Cross in 2008 proved a remarkable counterpart to the brief, thirteenth-century poem about Mary at the foot of the cross.

Contemporary lyrics of courtly love shape the background for our second medieval poem. As it has come down to us, it has no name. Some rightly suggest calling the poem "Christ's Love-Song." Christ presents himself as the Knight-Lover, the One who is driven by love for each human being: for "thee," repeated four times in the closing stanza. Let us see the poem and then comment further.

> Love me brought,/And love me wrought,/Man, to be thy
> fere [mate].
> Love me fed/And love me led/And love me lettet [allows]
> here.
>
> Love me slew,/And love me drew,/And love me laid on
> bier.

Love is my peace;/For love I chese [chose],/Man to buyen
dear.

No dread thee nought,/I have thee sought,/ Bothen day
and night,
To haven thee,/Well is me,/I have thee won in fight.

From a formal point of view, the reader must be struck by
the many monosyllables used in the three stanzas. In this lyric
that contains only seventy-three words, some monosyllabic
words recur in a powerful and direct fashion: "love" (ten times),
"me" (nine times), "thee" (four times), and "I" (three times).

The poem opens with God the Father, who is personified
love or love personified. It was the Father who "wrought" the
Son and "brought" him to become and remain the "fere" (loving mate) of every human being. As the poem goes on, the activity and suffering of Christ himself becomes clearer. Because of
his love he chose to "buyen dear" the human race.

This "buying dear" should not be understood to be a
"commercial" transaction that involved a high price literally
paid to someone (for instance, the devil) or to something (for
instance, some higher law). Rather it was the act of redeeming
humankind that cost Christ the Knight-Lover a great deal. If
"slain" by love in a mystical, even erotic, sense he was also quite
literally slain because of the situation into which his love had
led him. Love involved him in being killed and laid on a bier.

Here the poem permits itself a savage image: "love me
drew." The reader may even be expected to think of someone
who has been hung, drawn, and quartered. A less savage sense
would be "love killed me and pulled me along the ground"—like
the dead Hector being dragged around the walls of Troy by
Achilles.

In either case the paradox comes through strongly.
Although slain, seemingly defeated, and laid out for burial, the

Knight-Lover has in fact won. A eucharistic acclamation puts the paradox equivalently: "Dying, you destroyed our death."

The risen Christ speaks and is satisfied at what his coming into the world and then his passion and death have won for him: "Well is me." He tenderly comforts the reader: there is no need to give way to feelings of sadness and dismay ("No dread thee nought"). Christ himself is deeply satisfied, and so too should be those whom he has redeemed.

No longer does he address "man" (the first two stanzas) but, in a more personal way, he speaks four times to "thee" in the closing stanza: "Both day and night I have sought thee, wanting to have thee. Now well is me because I have won thee in the fight."

Obviously too much commentary risks taking the heart out of these two exquisite poems from the Middle Ages. But if I have opened them up a little for readers and helped to evoke some feelings of grief and joy as they reflect on the dying and rising of Christ, in my own way I too can say, "Well is me."

Part Two

THE COMING AND MISSION OF JESUS

1

The Annunciation

Our lives are patterned by events that are graced, hidden, unexpected, and sometimes decisive. All these possibilities emerge from St. Luke's account of the Annunciation (1:26–38), that moment when the human history of Jesus began.

Treasured by many generations of artists from Beato Angelico down to Andy Warhol, the story of the Annunciation has much to contribute toward renewing our Christian lives. I can think of four challenging and enriching themes to be drawn from the account in Luke.

First of all, the Annunciation brought the offer of a unique, personal favor to Mary: that she should become the mother of the Son of God. This was a marvelous grace for her personally but not a grace for her alone. The child she would conceive and bear was to reign forever over Israel and over the whole world. Mary exemplifies supremely how human beings, by accepting a remarkable gift for themselves, receive it also for others. Through Mary's "yes," the Son of God came to save the human race and the power of the Holy Spirit overshadowed the world.

This principle holds true for each of us. Whenever we allow ourselves to be led by the Holy Spirit into opening ourselves to the divine initiatives, we do this for others and never for ourselves alone. God's offers do not come as privileges for our private selves but also as public responsibilities. To the degree that we are constantly ready to accept personal favors from God, then through us the Son of God will come with greater intensity to save human beings, and a greater power of the Holy Spirit will overshadow our race and the world.

A second theme emerges from the "hidden" face of the Annunciation. It is a quiet, even secret event, even more unnoticed than the birth of Jesus would be. No shepherds, multitude of angels, or wise men from the East attend the event of the Annunciation. Not even St. Joseph is there. The "actors" are only two: Mary herself and the angel Gabriel.

Yet, as many poets and preachers have insisted, this hidden act on the part of Mary in saying "yes" to the divine plan was the most decisive action ever performed by a mere human being. The actions of Mary's Son would come from someone who was not only fully human but also truly divine. As the act of someone who was a "mere" human being, Mary's "let it be done as you have said" stands uniquely alone. Nothing will ever surpass or even compare with the consequences it initiated.

This suggests pondering further something that might already have occurred to us when we reflect on our own experiences. At times quiet, unnoticed actions can turn out to be most important. Apparently unimpressive acts, even totally secret ones, may enjoy a remarkable impact. A sincere decision to commit ourselves to a program of regular prayer may take place in the secrecy of our minds and hearts and pass totally unnoticed in the outside world. But its results may be spectacularly valuable for ourselves and for innumerable others.

Thirdly, many painters have depicted Mary as praying and quietly reflecting over the Scriptures—engaged in her *lectio divina*, if you like—at the moment of the Annunciation. Gabriel came on the scene with dramatic suddenness to bring an unexpected offer from God. Mary was invited to make a snap decision. But she was not caught wrong-footed. From the time of her own conception and birth, her whole life had been a preparation for this meeting. She had never literally practiced or rehearsed the scene of the Annunciation. But her holy and faithful life had been a perfect preparation for this moment.

Dramatic and unexpected moments of decision can also turn up in our own lives. They are those unrehearsed episodes when it may seem that the whole of our life comes into focus. For good or evil, our decision shows us up. We cannot practice the precise chance that opens up before us. We have no guarantee and firm security that we will react appropriately. Yet, if we faithfully seek to follow the will of God in all the ups and downs of life, there is much less danger that some unexpected moment of opportunity will find us lacking. Steady fidelity will enable us to respond wholeheartedly in the grace of the moment.

Fourthly and finally, the story of the Annunciation reaches its high point with Mary's acceptance: "I am the Lord's servant." We believe and know that Mary did not simply bring herself to say "yes" in one great moment alone. She kept up that "yes" constantly: from the Annunciation, through Bethlehem and Cana, and on to Calvary and the first Pentecost. Her entire existence formed a single, unbreakably faithful and strong piece. Her "yes" to God characterized her whole life before and after the Annunciation.

In our own lives we may be able to nerve ourselves to say "yes" to God at different moments and take some decisive step in serving God. But to keep that decision going through a lifetime is another thing. We must all hope and pray that the Blessed Virgin will "pray for us sinners," so that a touch of her loyal fidelity will rub off on all of us.

2

In Praise of Christmas Cards

Christmas is the only season of the year when many Christians regularly send each other pictures that express their faith. Three scenes predominate. The images may depict the Christ Child in the arms of Mary, the visit of the shepherds to the manger in Bethlehem, or else the coming of the exotic Magi with their gifts of gold, frankincense, and myrrh.

Some Christmas cards reproduce classical or modern representations of the Madonna and Child. In this category, works of Renaissance artists like Raphael frequently predominate. They have excelled themselves at depicting this most beautiful child, whose beauty is mirrored by the beauty of his mother as she holds him in her arms or gazes on him with intense love. Or the cards may show us the gently contemplative *Adoration of the Shepherds* by Giorgione or some other Italian master. These pictures quietly invite the viewer to join the shepherds in absorbing the wonderful truth of Christ's birth. Or else the cards bring us an elaborate and enchanting *Adoration of the Magi* by Botticelli or Fra Filippo Lippi. They show us angels joining a cavalcade of human beings in celebrating exuberantly the human birth of the Son of God.

Those of us who receive many cards at Christmas put them on mantelpieces in a sitting room, or cover a kitchen wall with them, or else string them on cords along corridors. We check our lists carefully to make sure that the friends and relatives who have sent us a card have already received one from us.

However, we might also take a little time to gaze prayerfully at each of the cards and let the concentrated intensity of their visual art come alive for us. What we see in Christmas cards can take on a special, even an intense, significance.

Whenever we begin to appreciate deeply someone or something for ourselves, we are often prompted to do so by what we see, perhaps for the first time: on a TV screen, in a book, at work, along a street, in our home, in church, or across a crowded room. What does visual art, in particular religious art, do to us? Contemplated quietly when seen perhaps for the first time, this art can become a *window* into Christ and a *mirror* of ourselves.

Some of the Renaissance masterpieces place Christ's manger in beautiful landscapes. But any landscape is only the background to the story of Jesus, Mary, Joseph, the shepherds, and the Magi—not to mention the angelic visitors who turn up and put the whole story into a cosmic setting. The masterpieces reproduced on our Christmas cards form a window into the intimate and beautiful story of the coming of the Christ Child and the response of heaven and earth to his birth—the shorter journey of the local shepherds and the longer journey of the Magi from the East. Our Christmas cards offer us a window into the life of others, all those who respond with faith and love to the Baby lying in the manger or enfolded by the arms of Mary.

Some of the Christmas paintings open a window onto the spiritual journeys of believers down through the ages. Artists over the centuries have introduced into their scenes of the nativity later Christians, both saints and sinners, men and women dressed in the clothes of their times and cultures. These pictures let us see something of the story of how Christians of all ages have responded to the birth of Jesus.

Contemplating the scenes that our Christmas cards depict is a two-way affair. They are not only windows into the wider history of faith, but they are also mirrors that can put embarrassing questions to us. They invite us to think back to Christmas plays at our schools, where we may have taken the role of a shepherd, of a king or, if we were really lucky, of Joseph, or even of Mary herself. Does the Christ Child still fill our hearts with joy? Has Jesus born at the first Christmas continued to be the greatest value in our lives, the very center of our existence? Yes, Christmas cards work as windows that show us who Jesus is. But they also hold up mirrors of our own story and remind us of who we are and where we have arrived on the pilgrimage though life.

Spending a little time contemplating Christmas cards can easily become a self-involving exercise, a meeting between Jesus and ourselves, and a chance of experiencing something of his enchanting beauty. To be sure, many contemporary Christmas cards do not supply us with fully deployed and beautiful pictures from the nativity story. They may carry an uncomplicated message: "A Merry Christmas and a Happy New Year," "Peace on Earth," or merely one word, "Peace." Some cards display symbols like a star, a pair of angels blowing trumpets, a candle, or a Christmas tree. Yet there can still be a simple beauty there, provided the lines are well drawn and the letters made with elegant loveliness.

Whether they bear classical or modern images, straightforward symbols, or merely words, Christmas cards aim to be beautiful. Even very ordinary ones let through something of the lovely Christ Child. We all need to feel the impact of that beauty. To echo and adapt some famous words from Dostoevsky, it is the beauty of Christ and only his beauty that will save the world. We are led through his beauty to grasp the deep truth of his coming and lead the lives of goodness and justice that he desires.

Experience repeatedly shows how the presence and power of beauty persistently provide a remedy for the sense of meaninglessness that plagues so many lives. Falling in love with some beautiful person liberates us from chaotic wanderings and brings order and direction to our lives. Beauty illuminates and transforms. Charles Dickens's *Christmas Carol* shows how beauty and goodness change the hard heart of old Scrooge, as well as touching those who read the book or see versions of it on the screen or stage. A truly beautiful story can deliver us from a self-absorbed existence and give fresh meaning and shape to our own stories.

In their own modest way, Christmas cards open the door to Christ, his beauty and his uniquely beautiful story. His beauty comes to us as a wonderful gift from God. The beautiful Christ Child invites us to open ourselves up to him, become flooded with delight, stay in his lovely presence, and let the impact of his unparalleled beauty shape our whole existence now and forever.

It is worth taking Christmas cards down from our mantelpieces and kitchen walls to hold them in our hands and quietly let them prompt a heart-to-heart conversation with Jesus. They can give us access to him and a renewed sense of his unique beauty. When they do that, Christmas cards will turn out to be the best of any presents we might receive from our dearest friends and relatives.

3
Kissed into Life

Some years ago at Christmas, a little cousin of mine was playing the role of Sleeping Beauty with her grandfather. There she was pretending to be asleep because, like the princess in the story, she had pricked her finger on the poisoned spindle. Her grandfather tiptoed over to the couch were she was lying. He kissed once and then twice. But nothing happened. She did not stir.

"I kissed you twice," he said to his granddaughter. Without opening her eyes, little Charlotte said: "You have to kiss me three times. I've pricked my finger three times on the poisoned spindle."

We all need to be kissed into life—not just twice or three times, but many, many times. The kiss of love brings us to life, and keeps us alive. Without love we do not really live. When we receive love, we can live and grow and laugh.

We have probably all seen how love can bring people alive. They may have gone on for years without receiving much love, and then someone gives them the love they so desperately need. Like Sleeping Beauty, they can come alive in a wonderful, new way.

We have all pricked our fingers on various poisoned spindles. We need love, God's limitless love, to wake us up and let us live fully and truly. God is greater than even the best of grandfathers and grandmothers.

As the year draws to a close and the feast of the nativity comes around, we might remember little Charlotte and think of

Christmas differently this coming December. Christmas is God's way of kissing us and opening our eyes again to life.

When my little cousin was playing at being Sleeping Beauty, her grandfather had to kiss her and wake her up. At Christmas it is the other way round. It is the baby Jesus himself, God's loving gift, who kisses us and helps us live and live in wonderfully new ways. Do let the Christ Child kiss you this coming Christmas.

4

The Face of the Christ Child

Every human face is thoroughly special; it belongs to *that* unique individual. Faces live on in our memories and hearts; a face "across a crowded room" may change our lives forever.

Before a baby is born, parents, relatives, and friends long to see its face. Once it is born, they find so much to interpret and cherish in the tiny features of its face. As the child grows up, they want to see how its face grows and subtly changes.

Shortly after I began living in Rome in 1974, two young friends, a young musical composer and his wife, asked me to baptize their first child, a daughter they named Chiara Francesca. Every other week after her birth, I was with that baby, and watched her eyes open and her face come alive. I saw her begin to smile and shine upon those around her. The tiny child lit up the faces of her parents and the faces of strangers on the street, people in church, and men and women sitting at other tables in Roman restaurants. Her vivid and smiling face put smiles on their faces and joy in their hearts.

What Chiara Francesca did many years ago in Rome spoke to me again and again of another baby, the Christ Child, who came to put smiles on the faces of all human beings.

In a lovely prayer the psalmist tells of his heart seeking the face of God: "It is your face, O Lord, that I seek; hide not your face from me" (Ps 27:8–9). Centuries later a dramatic answer to that prayer came when "the glory of God" shone on "the face of Christ" (2 Cor 4:6). Christ is the face of God come amongst us, or—more briefly—the human face of God.

The opening chapters of the Gospels according to Matthew and Luke bring us a cast of holy people who were seeking the face of God: above all, Mary and Joseph. God did not hide his face from them. The Baby they took in their arms showed them nothing less than the human face of God. For that unique couple, Mary and Joseph, the prayer of the psalmist came true. They were the first human beings to gaze upon the face of the incarnate Son of God. When his eyes opened and he began to smile upon them, they knew the first appearance on earth of the very glory of God.

Matthew and Luke tell us of others who also looked upon the face of the Christ Child and found great joy in experiencing that grace: the shepherds, the wise men from the East, Simeon and Anna.

They stood in for all of us who walk in darkness and live in deep shadows. We too have seen a great light on the face of the Baby in Mary's arms. That child has been born for us and that son has been given to us so that his face might shine upon us. This child has come to scatter darkness, to fill all human hearts with happiness, and to light up faces everywhere. His coming was and remains forever news of very great joy to be shared by all peoples.

After so many years I remember what Chiara Francesca did to people along the streets of Rome. She brought me a wonderful truth. Jesus was born so that men and women might look on his baby face and smile. We know that this was indeed the human face of our gloriously beautiful God.

5
The Greatest Love Story

When the musical *Gone with the Wind* opened in 2007, it was advertised as "the greatest love story ever told." Sadly the musical fell well below the level of the novel and the movie on which it was based. But could you call even the novel and the movie "the greatest love story ever told"?

All power to *Gone with the Wind*, but I would rather say that the story of Jesus is the greatest love story ever told. What makes the story of Jesus just that? What might we say about the love revealed in the whole story of Jesus?

To reply adequately to those questions would take days, weeks, and actually a whole lifetime. Love proves itself to be an incredibly rich and many-sided reality. The classic Italian poet Dante Alighieri spent his entire life exploring and portraying love—human love and divine love. We too pass our lifetimes coming to appreciate ever more deeply what Christ's love for us means and what our love for one another should truly be.

So we face a gigantic theme and enduring challenge when we read those words from St. John's Gospel, "...I shall love them and reveal myself to them" (John 14:21). What does Jesus mean by loving us and revealing himself to us?

His words recall one central feature of authentic love: its transparency and its willingness to share and to share with total honesty. Jesus is totally transparent with us. He wants to show himself to us and share his deepest reality with each one of us.

Real love is always like that. True lovers constantly want to open up, to show their deep selves, and to share all the secrets of their hearts with those whom they love. True lovers want to be utterly transparent with each other.

Jesus is our true lover, utterly transparent with us, always wanting to show himself to us, and to share himself with us. We spend our whole life with Jesus loving us, showing himself to us in so many ways, and sharing himself with us constantly. To each of us he is always saying: "I love you and I want to reveal myself to you and to share myself with you."

Long live that great love story, *Gone with the Wind*. But the greatest love story is the story of Jesus. Both in this life and in the life to come, he is driven by his love for us. Both here and hereafter, he wants nothing else than the chance of loving us, showing himself to us, and sharing himself with us for ever and ever.

6

What Was Jesus Like?

How did Jesus come across to those who met him in the few, packed years of his ministry? Certainly not as a kind of "superman" who was never weary. He was remembered as once being so worn out that he even fell asleep in a boat during a storm. He was pictured as being so tired from a journey that he sat exhausted by a well and asked a stranger for a cup of water to drink. None of the Gospels suggest that miracles supplied him with superhuman energy, let alone food and drink. He was very different from those people we sometimes meet who are bursting with energy, never betray any weariness, and seem capable of living in a constant frenzy of activity.

Some critics harshly dismissed Jesus as "a glutton and a drunkard, a friend of tax collectors and sinners" (Luke 7:34). That was a nasty sneer, but all the same it expressed something profoundly true about Jesus and his habits. For him, eating and drinking with others provided a way of entering into communion with all kinds of people, especially those with serious, spiritual problems. They found him to be a wonderful friend to be with, someone who never turned dysfunctional people away and who changed their lives—often by taking meals with them.

Years ago a book about Jesus was published with the marvelous title, *Jesus in Bad Company*. Yes, that was where you often found him. He looked for the marginalized and even criminal members of society. He reached out to sinners and not least to hated tax collectors, those who collaborated with the occupying army and extorted unreasonable amounts of money out of ordinary citizens. Jesus welcomed such unsavory people, shared meals with them, and did his best to meet their spiritual needs.

Self-righteous people dismissed Jesus as a "party boy," who did not know how to behave like a proper prophet. This criticism implied, however, something profoundly true. The Old Testament prophets and Jesus' immediate precursor, John the Baptist, all longed to bring sinners to repent and give up their evil ways. But none of them ever tried to do that, as Jesus did, by sharing table fellowship with sinful men and women. He stood apart from his prophetic predecessors by turning meals into a means of healing people and forming a lasting friendship with them. Those meals were to reach their climax on the night before he died, when he used a meal to institute the Eucharist and create a sacred eating and drinking as *the* way for transforming lives and establishing a deep communion with sinners for ever and ever.

Jesus shared the central joys of human living. John's Gospel tells of him taking part in a marriage feast and miraculously supplying wine when it ran short (John 2:1-11). To be sure, that story carries a lovely symbolic message. Jesus changed the water used for rites of purification into the new wine of the final kingdom of God—a sign that revealed how he was replacing the old order with a transformed world. But let us not forget the primary thrust of the miracle: it allowed all the guests at the wedding to continue their celebration.

No impassive, unemotional figure, Jesus could react angrily at intolerable situations. His eyes blazed with anger at those who wanted to stop him helping a disabled person (Mark 3:1-6). He ran wild in the Temple, when he found traders and money changers defiling the holiness of God's house. He flung down their tables and drove them there and then out of the precincts (Mark 11:15-17). Tears came to his eyes over the failure of Jerusalem to repent and hear his message of peace (Luke 19:41). He wept too at the death of his friend Lazarus (John 11:35).

Jesus was clearly hurt when he "failed" to meet the expectations of those close to him, like Peter (Mark 8:32–33) and members of his own family and hometown (Mark 3:21; 6:1–6). He had to endure outrageous taunts over his work in liberating from the power of Satan those diabolically possessed. Some cultured critics acknowledged the facts but claimed that he could exorcise the possessed because he was in league with the ruler of the demons (Mark 3:22). He feared, according to John's Gospel, that the core group of the Twelve might leave him in the aftermath of his discourse on the bread of life: "Will you also go away?" (John 6:67).

When his violent death drew near, Jesus did not behave like a tough, cool hero. In deep distress he pleaded with his heavenly Father: "All things are possible for you. Remove this chalice from me." He bargained with his God before accepting the divine will: "...not what I want but what you want" (Mark 14:33–36).

In his letters, St. Paul has little to say about table fellowship with sinners, miracles, teaching, and further features of the public ministry of Jesus; he leaves it to others to hand on what the eyewitnesses had experienced during Jesus' life. That makes it all the more precious when the apostle sums up the story of Jesus: "He did not please himself" (Rom 15:3). Putting this positively, we could say that Jesus went out of his way to meet the needs of others. There was a straight line from the ministry of Jesus to his death on the cross: from the beginning to the end, he forgot himself and gave his life away for all those he came to serve.

The Gospel of John constantly presents Jesus acting with great purposefulness. He moved without hesitation because he gave total priority to the will of his Father. That resolute obedience gave Jesus a sustained strength and made his life unbreakably strong. The serene pursuit of the divine will was the secret at the heart of Jesus' whole existence, and also the reason why "many believed in him" (John 8:28–30).

7

Crazy About Jesus

Early in the twentieth century, films about Jesus made in Hollywood and elsewhere never showed his face. Later, when film directors like Franco Zeffirelli in *Jesus of Nazareth* started showing the face of Jesus, they normally picked very handsome men to play the role. These directors appreciated how wonderfully handsome and truly beautiful Jesus was. Even if the Gospels never directly describe Jesus, they support Zeffirelli and the other directors. During the ministry of Jesus people flocked to him, they were drawn to his presence, they gazed upon his face and, as Luke 19:48 says, "they all hung upon his words."

Beautiful people always attract us; we want to stay in their presence. We never tire of listening to them; their words speak to our hearts. We fall in love with people who are beautiful. That is the normal impact of beauty. It touches our hearts and fills us with joy. That is just what the beautiful Jesus did: he spoke to the hearts of people and filled them with joy. They fell in love with him.

Just before Christmas 1999, the Italian national television transmitted a film on Jesus that they had made in collaboration with an American group. The film was simply called *Jesus*. However you judged the film or compared it, for instance, with Zeffirelli's *Jesus of Nazareth*, this later film brought out one very central item: Jesus was immensely attractive to all kinds of people. The young and the old, men and women, the sick and the healthy, farmers and city folk—all found him to be stunningly beautiful. They were crazy about him and swarmed around him. That film *Jesus* captured a key truth about Jesus and his story: people experienced him as radiantly attractive and they flocked to his presence.

The film *Jesus* took you through the life, death, and resurrection of Jesus, and then finished by doing something intriguing and interesting. It jumped forward two thousand years and pictured Jesus in jeans on the waterfront in Malta. As he stood there in the port of Valletta, a whole bunch of small children ran toward him: forty or fifty of them, from little ones who were only three or four years of age up to twelve- or thirteen-year-old kids. All of them obviously found him so lovely and simply wanted to be with him. Jesus picked up one tiny child and walked off, with the infant in his arms and all the others following him. The beautiful Jesus exited with the beautiful children.

Some years ago I baptized Maymie, the tiny daughter of two dear friends who lived in London. At the baptism, I said: "Maymie, like the rest of us, will have only one go at life. I hope and pray that she will make a marvelous go at life. She will do that if she finds in Jesus someone who is uniquely lovely, someone whom she will always cherish. Right here and now Jesus cherishes her with an infinite love. As she grows up, may she always experience Jesus as someone stunningly beautiful and uniquely attractive—someone she will always be happy to be with. It is his love that will enable her to find in him the One who satisfies the deepest longings of all our hearts."

8
The Miracle of Growth

One of life's special blessings for me was the chance of growing up on a farm. Those early years taught me to be astonished by the mystery of new life: fluffy chickens darting across the ground ahead of hens; fresh, white rings of flowers on pear trees; wild rabbits enjoying the grass on an early summer's evening. I still feel a thrill of wonder when I recall all that growth: cows licking their newborn calves; sharp-eyed magpies strutting around with their young; peas and beans shooting up where I had planted seeds in the vegetable garden.

Once I started to read the Gospels seriously, it made me happy to find how often Jesus drew his images from farming. He knew that donkeys and oxen needed to be taken out each day to drink water. Those farm animals could at times fall down wells and needed to be rescued even on the sacred day of rest. Jesus recalled how barren fig trees might be revitalized by cultivating the soil around them and adding a little manure. He had learned to predict what is very important for farmers: the weather. Winds from the west blew off the Mediterranean and brought rain; the winds from the south came in from the desert and would be hot and dry. Minding sheep, ploughing the land, sowing seed, and other farming activities turned up constantly in the preaching of Jesus.

In a special way, what caught his eye was the marvel of seeds. They send up shoots, and slowly but surely produce crops, bushes, and trees. He drew on this experience to make up stories that continue to speak to us about God's powerful rule establishing itself in our world. Through his stories taken from things that grow on farms, Jesus encouraged his audience to have utter confidence in the power of God to bring about the new and wonderful life of the divine kingdom.

Many good things of the kingdom are happening right now, and many more are on the way. Jesus wanted us to look at our gardens, our orchards, and our fields. They can help us recognize how, quietly and powerfully, God makes everything grow, bloom, and ripen in our world and in our lives.

Jesus, I believe, would have been delighted by a natural phenomenon that occurs every few years in Australia. A monsoon swings off-course and dumps tons of water across the dry, desert land. Within a few weeks, under the blazing sun, plants spring up, flowers bloom, birds return, and the deep mud under previously dried-up lakes produces fish in abundance. The dead heart of Australia comes alive. What can happen in that desert vividly suggests the life and growth that God gives everywhere.

Jesus drew from his experience of farming and the sowing of seeds to tell his stories about growth. He wanted to suggest a growth that is beyond our understanding and control, as the divine energy works in our world.

His stories about the sowing and growth of seeds always take me back to my childhood. In the freshness of the morning, I would run out into the vegetable garden and find shoots sprouting through the soil where I had planted seeds. Some days later, rows of beans and peas stood up cheerfully in the sunlight. Vital energy was at work, even though I did not know how. God was offering me a lesson about growth and vital increase in the divine kingdom.

That growth is at work, and goes beyond our understanding and control. Things may look dead. But trust Jesus and the power of God. Beyond our understanding and beyond our control, the divine energy is at work and will bring its astonishing results.

9

Jesus and the Call to Love

Many years ago I was reading some reflections on loving others by a well-known theologian. A few pages into the article I found him claiming that, without Christ, we simply would not know how far our love should extend. Still less would we be able to practice the love required of us. At the time this claim seemed somewhat exaggerated to me. But then I came across two things that made me realize the theologian had a case after all: a letter to a paper in the North of England and some remarks by Sigmund Freud.

The letter turned up in a controversy involving a Christian and an atheist humanist. The Christian remarked that his atheist opponent should at least read the basic documents. The following week the atheist in question replied by saying that he had bought a copy of the New Testament and had started to read from the beginning. But when he reached chapter 5 of Matthew's Gospel, he put away the New Testament as "hippie nonsense." He had come up against the injunction: "Love your enemies."

In his *Civilization and Its Discontents*, Freud quotes what he calls "the grandiose commandment," "You shall love your neighbor as yourself," and asks: "Why should I do it? How can it be possible?" "If I am to love someone," Freud continues, "he must deserve it in some way. But so many men don't." Freud adds that if the commandment ran, "Love your neighbor as your neighbor loves you," he would not take exception to it, but as the commandment stands, he finds it unreasonable and impossible to fulfill. In their different ways, the atheist letter-writer and Freud remind us that the commandment of love is not nearly as obvious and easy as we might come to think it is.

The Good Samaritan Story

A startling parable about love that Jesus told in response to a lawyer's question shows something of the challenge involved in pinning down love and putting it into practice (Luke 10:25–37). With his question "Who is my neighbor?" the lawyer tried to pin down in advance what love demands. Seemingly he wanted from Jesus a precise statement about the people who make up the category of "my neighbors." He seemed to have expected Jesus to list certain classes of people and omit others, or perhaps to mention certain kinds of events when love should be exercised and to omit other kinds of events when there would be no call to practice love. Instead Jesus told him a story about a man in terrible need and the way in which three people reacted to that need. "My neighbor" cannot be legislated about or precisely defined in advance. He or she is anyone at all who needs, perhaps desperately needs, my help.

The parable also hints at a precondition for exercising love. First the priest and then the Levite, we read, passed by "on the other side." They refused to stop and *look* at the man who had been robbed and badly wounded by bandits. They turned their eyes away. The Samaritan, however, *saw* the wounded traveler, had compassion on him, and interrupted his journey to provide the necessary intensive care. Our eyes are the gate-ways of compassion. If we do not notice some pain or misery that tears apart the life of our neighbor, we will not stop to help. The precondition for doing something is the willingness to *look at* others who are suffering.

Different Answers to the Same Question?

When he initiates the dialogue that leads Jesus to tell the story of the Good Samaritan, the lawyer begins with the question: "Good Master, what must I *do* to inherit eternal life?" The whole encounter ends with Jesus telling him, "Go and *do* likewise"—that is to say, "Go and act as the Samaritan acted (italics mine)." Some chapters later there is another encounter, this time with a rich man, which begins with the same question: "Good Teacher, what must I do to win eternal life?" That encounter ends with Jesus inviting the man, "Come, follow me" (Luke 18:18–23).

The same question produces two seemingly different (even mutually exclusive) answers, the first directing someone to care for anyone he meets in desperate need and the second inviting the questioner to join Jesus and become his disciple. The first time Jesus replies by saying "go" and the second time he says "come."

Putting this issue in the context of the two volumes produced by St. Luke, his Gospel and the Book of Acts, attentive readers will notice how this evangelist repeatedly presents "doublets" or two stories that complement each other and work to give a more complete picture. Thus the two stories we have just examined are intimately connected. To follow the Son of God is to care for the brother or sister in need. The service of the neighbor in need and following Jesus are radically linked. "Going and doing likewise" involve "coming and following me," and vice versa. Inheriting eternal life entails hearing and accepting the double invitation.

Mark and John

In the Gospel of Mark Jesus makes the same point, albeit in a slightly different way. A scribe asks him: "Which commandment is the first of all?" He receives the obvious answer: "...you shall love the Lord your God with your whole heart and with your whole soul, and with all your mind and with all your strength." But then, of his own accord, Jesus adds: "The second commandment is this. You shall love your neighbor as yourself" (Mark 12:28–31). In other words, talk about loving God is a delusion unless it involves us also in loving our neighbor.

The First Letter of John supports this conclusion, but in a surprising way: "If God has so loved us, we ought to love one another" (1 John 4:11). This seems a paradoxical conclusion. Strict logic would lead us to expect: "If God has so loved us, we ought to love God." What St. John means is that when we love our neighbor, we are in fact loving God.

No one in their right mind questions the centrality of love in the Gospels and the rest of the New Testament. But it is open to question whether Christians have always grasped how difficult and total is the love that Jesus requires. John remarks: "By this we know love, that he [Jesus] laid down his love for us; and we ought to lay down our lives for our brothers and sisters" (1 John 3:16). Here John is repeating the message from Jesus in the last discourse: "This is the greatest love people can show, that they should lay down their lives for their friends" (John 15:13).

Every now and then the call to make such a sacrifice becomes a reality. During the Second World War, the father of a friend of mine stayed behind on an island to care for the sick in hospital, although he could have been evacuated with the other civilians. This doctor paid for his love with his life. The enemy forces arrived and executed him. Many of us will have stories like that to tell: of pastors refusing to abandon high-crime areas and eventually paying for their devotion with their lives; of nurses stopping to care for a wounded person shot by some crazed young man and then being gunned down themselves; of aid workers coming home in a coffin. Authentic love always makes itself vulnerable; for the sake of others, it is willing to face rejection, danger, and even death.

The Example of Love

Christianity offers us not merely a code of love but a supreme example of love, that love revealed in the life and death of Jesus himself. His love was an *active* love, one that wanted to cross the distance between God and human beings and reach out to us, even when we did not know him and were as yet sinners. Are we ready to cross the distance between ourselves and others and, like Jesus, to reach out to others who do not care for us and perhaps do not even know us?

Christians are called to take the initiative in their loving. Even before offering their "gifts at the altar," they should go and be reconciled with those they have offended (Matt 5:23–24). Like the Good Samaritan, they should stop for their wounded brothers and sisters and take care of them. Jesus expects them to visit the sick and welcome the stranger. Their love should not wait for its cue but should act spontaneously when faced with those in distress. This is a love that is quick to see just how much misery and frustration can be concealed behind the faces of others.

Christ's love was active and also supremely *unselfish*. He was "the man born to give." In the words of the Acts of the Apostles, "he went about doing good" (Acts 10:38). It was the great Swiss theologian Karl Barth who first contrasted Jesus with the rest of us by saying that he was "a man *for* others" and we are "men *with* others." Following Christ means trying to shift from being merely people "with others" to become people "for others." Being disciples of Jesus calls on us to give others our time, our interest, and our loving friendship, and to do so without any eye on some return. It is all too easy to drift into living as if his love command ran: "Love your neighbor as your neighbor loves you." To test ourselves, it can be worthwhile even now and then to go out of our way and do some loving action for which there could be no possible return.

Being active and unselfish, Christian love is also necessarily a very *practical* love. Often the practice of love may call for something as simple and yet as profound as a few loving words —even as straightforward as saying to someone, "I love you."

Or it may be something muted but none the less expressive, like the words with which Rod Steiger says good-bye at the end of an Oscar-winning film, *In The Heat of the Night*: "Virgil, you take care." Steiger, playing the role of a prejudiced but shrewd country sheriff, has been investigating a murder. At the railway station he arrests a well-dressed, black stranger who turns out to be a top homicide detective from Philadelphia, played by Sidney Poitier. The two men work together to solve the murder and grow in mutual esteem. Much feeling and even love are conveyed by those words of farewell, "Virgil, you take care."

Our words have the power to touch and change human lives. They can spread hate and wickedness or love, hope, and joy. Nobody can experience being loved and remain the same. Love always seeks the right word, a word of love.

We can combine what 1 John 4 tells us twice ("God is love") with the prologue of John's Gospel ("the Word was God") and say: "God so loved us that he gave us his Word of love." In our case, if we love others, we will give them our word of love, the word that lifts their burden and breathes the breath of life into them. As much or even more than truth, love will set people free (see John 8:32).

Years ago I came across a poster that announced: "Without love you won't get very far." "That doesn't go to the heart of the matter," I thought. "Surely, without love you won't get anywhere at all."

The Good Innkeeper

The great parable of love puts at the center the Samaritan and his love that is supremely practical. He breaks his journey to give his time and total attention to the wounded traveler. He uses what he has to tend to the man's wounds—the wine to serve as a cleansing antiseptic and the oil to soften the wounds. But let us not forget the Judean innkeeper in whose care the wounded person is left. With his unquestioning hospitality, the innkeeper not only trusts the Samaritan to return and pay any extra expenses but also fits into a theme that punctuates the Gospel of Luke. This Gospel opens with an inn (a *kataluma* in Greek) in Bethlehem where there was no place for Mary and Joseph (2:7), and ends with a Jerusalem inn (22:11; also *kataluma*) where Jesus celebrated the Passover and instituted the Eucharist on the night before he died. In Luke's Gospel, the life of Christ stretches between an inn where he failed to receive welcome on the occasion of his birth and that inn in Jerusalem where, a few hours before he was arrested, he showed the most exquisite hospitality to his friends. Between the inn at the beginning and the inn at the end, Jesus told a most powerful parable that featured a truly hospitable innkeeper.

This subtheme in Luke's Gospel could encourage us to say that love is being a good innkeeper. Love is a hospitality that makes everyone welcome. So often love is simply that—being a good host.

The love that Jesus encouraged and embodied is startlingly radical. It calls for a moral revolution. The followers of Jesus must dream of a world or at least of a community in which mutual love glows like bright, warm sunshine. This is not "hippie nonsense" but the dream of someone who "loved his own who were in the world and loved them to the very end" (John 13:1).

10
The Healing of Two Women
(Matt 9:18–26)

We have here an example of what Matthew often does with healing stories when he takes them over from the first Gospel, that of Mark: he shortens drastically what he finds in Mark. To tell the story of the healing of two persons, Mark needs twenty-three verses (Mark 5:21–43). Matthew cuts it all down to nine verses, much less than half of what Mark needs to tell it all.

Yet Matthew keeps the essence of the story about two women who are healed: one, a grown woman who had suffered from constant bleeding for twelve years; and the other, a girl of twelve who fell ill and then died.

Because of her bleeding, the woman was regarded by Jewish law as permanently unclean. She was socially and religiously marginalized, a kind of pariah shunned by her society. In a word, she was socially and religiously *dead*. The little girl suffered a physical *death*. She was cut off from her family and friends when she fell sick and then died. For both women, Jesus came on the scene and radically changed a deadly situation for each of them.

By curing her hemorrhage, Jesus brought the woman back from her social and religious death. He then brought the young girl back to her family and friends by raising her from the dead.

Neither Matthew nor his source, Mark, tell us the names of the two women. In the Gospel texts they both remain anonymous. Yet their lives were rescued from anonymity. Around the world, year by passing year, those who celebrate the Eucharist remember their story when it is read at the Eucharist. They are remembered and cherished, because on a certain day they both met Jesus, one after the other, and their lives were changed forever.

One of them met Jesus because she went looking for him and touched his cloak. The other was far too sick to leave her bed. Her father went looking for Jesus, and he came to her. It does not matter very much how the two women encountered Jesus. What matters is that they did meet him. Meeting Jesus changed their lives for all time. Two thousand years later they are recalled when Christians read the Gospels and celebrate the Eucharist.

Few women who read or hear this passage in Matthew suffer, like the first woman in his story, from permanent menstrual bleeding. None of those who read or hear the passage will have died and be lying stretched out dead like the twelve-year-old girl. But in other ways we are all ill and desperately need Jesus and his healing touch. He is always there to heal our sick and deadly situations, and to change our lives forever.

It does not matter very much how we meet him. What matters is that we do meet him, day by day. Meeting him, meeting him over and over again, changes our lives. Jesus is always there for us—to heal us and lift us constantly from all the deadly situations that afflict us. He is nothing less than our true healer and our constant friend.

11
Comforts and Challenges (Luke 14:12–14)

During his years of teaching, Jesus said some very comforting things but he also said many challenging things. He offered comfort: "Come to me all you who labor and are heavily burdened, and I will give you rest." But he also made challenging demands: "When you give a lunch or a dinner, do not ask your friends, brothers, relatives, or rich neighbours. No, when you put on a party, invite the poor, the crippled, the lame, and the blind."

The crippled, the lame, and the blind form a clearly defined group. They are those who suffer permanently from some serious physical disability. "The poor" make up a much broader group. They are all those who, in various ways, suffer injustice and remain destitute. They are those who cannot defend themselves and often have no one to protect them or care for them.

Jesus challenges us with these words: "Invite the poor, the crippled, the lame, and the blind." His challenge recalls a remark from G. K. Chesterton: "Christianity hasn't been tried and found wanting. It's been found hard and not tried." And yet in this case, I think, Chesterton went too far. Some Catholics and other Christians hear the message of Jesus and do invite the poor, the crippled, the lame, and the blind.

When Pope John Paul II beatified Mother Teresa of Calcutta in 2003, television networks carried that ceremony in Rome around the world. The beatification provided a vivid instance of

Christians who accept the challenge of Jesus. Front seats in St. Peter's Square were reserved for 3,500 poor people. After Mass, they were invited to have lunch in the vast audience hall, where diplomats from the United Nations' Food and Agriculture Organization served the meal.

That was a mega example of accepting Jesus' request: "When you put on a party, invite the poor, the crippled, the lame, and the blind." Many simpler, more homely examples come to mind. Years ago, when I was studying at Cambridge University in England, I got to know a South African research scholar and his wife. At that time the streets of Cambridge featured numerous derelicts. Whenever beggars turned up at their door, the Stewarts would invite them in for a meal or at least a cup of tea and a sandwich.

In recent years I have been struck by the number of people in England who give up their normal Christmas to work in soup kitchens or offer their professional services free to those in great need. Instead of staying at home with family and friends, these people spend the days of Christmas serving the destitute.

Here I boldly suggest adding something to the teaching of Jesus. In the Gospel he says: "When you have a party, invite the poor, the crippled, the lame, and the blind. That they cannot pay you back means that you are fortunate, because repayment will be made to you when the virtuous rise again." I certainly do not want to query that wonderful promise. Those who serve the poor and the disabled are blessed and fortunate. God will repay them abundantly at the end, when they rise from the dead to the new and utterly worthwhile life to come. Yes, those who care for the destitute will be fully rewarded in the future.

Yet, also here and now, they are blessed and rewarded. They find, here and now, a special joy and satisfaction in caring for those who desperately need their help. They experience, right now, a particular happiness in obeying the call of Jesus to serve the poor. That was and is the experience of Mother Teresa and all those like her, who open their arms to the destitute, care for those who are physically disabled, and spend their days serving the less fortunate. Yes, the challenge of Jesus looks hard but it also brings its own special joy and happiness.

12

"Abiding in Me"

"Those who eat my flesh and drink my blood abide in me and I in them" (John 6:56).

These words come toward the end of the long discourse on the bread of life in chapter 6 of John's Gospel. It is a rich and inspiring chapter, and yet it may leave us a little disappointed. After all, it does not present us with the institution of the Eucharist. We may have the same feeling when we move ahead to the Last Supper and chapters 13 through 17 of John's Gospel. Where are the words about the Eucharist being instituted?

To be sure, John does not give us what we read in the other Gospels: the very words and actions of Jesus when instituting the Eucharist on the night before he died. But John's Gospel does provide us with some marvelous insights into the impact and value of the Eucharist.

Above all, the Eucharist means "abiding" in Christ and drawing life from him, a life that will last forever. Chapter 6 of John expresses the impact of the Eucharist as such a life-giving "abiding" in Christ, but does not give us some image or picture of what that might mean and look like. Such an image turns up in the last discourse: "I am the vine and you are the branches" (John 15:5).

Here the Gospel borrowed a familiar picture from what happened in the spring and early summer in ancient Palestine. The branches of vines sent out shoots and showed how they were full of life. They developed and spread vigorously to bear

---

eventually heavy bunches of grapes. That was and remains a lovely image of what the Eucharist brings about. We live, grow, and bear fruit, because we are the branches of Christ, the flourishing vine. A very familiar mosaic in the Roman church of San Clemente uses the symbol of the vine and branches to show how Christ nourishes and gives rich vitality to all who live and abide in him.

When I grew up in Australia, I was blessed by a family that included three priests. My uncles celebrated the Eucharist every day, and I often served their masses. But I learned more about the power of the Eucharist from another relative, Aunt Mary. Very soon after the birth of her second child, her marriage broke up. However, Mary enjoyed a very productive life, employed as a social worker and radio commentator for a large archdiocese.

In my earlier years I used to ask myself: where does Aunt Mary's vitality come from? Where does she find her strength and radiant joy? Then I discovered that she attended Mass on a daily basis. She drew from Christ her vitality, joy, and strength. For me, she served as living evidence of what Jesus meant by saying: "I am the vine and you are the branches." Aunt Mary proved a living example of what Jesus promises: "Those who eat my flesh and drink my blood abide in me and I in them."

May we all in our turn enjoy through the Eucharist a profound intimacy with Christ. Then we will draw life from the "Vine that is Life itself."

13

"Eating This Bread and Drinking This Cup"

Some time ago, I spent a week in the highlands of Scotland, giving lectures to some monks in a monastery founded in the Middle Ages, Pluscarden Abbey. A little more than sixty years ago the Benedictines returned, put a roof back on the ruins and again took up monastic life there. Sheltered by the high, stone walls of the chapel, they celebrate Mass looking up at a vast, modern stained-glass window of Christ. It depicts him holding in one hand some bread and in the other hand a chalice. Below him are representations of the wheat and grapes from which the bread and wine are made.

At the Last Supper Jesus took some bread and said: "This is my body that is for you." He then took a cup of wine and said: "This cup is the new covenant in my blood." When instituting the Eucharist, Jesus used something to be eaten and something to be drunk: some bread and some wine. His choice of the elements was affected, of course, by the setting of the Last Supper: the celebration of the Jewish Passover. Tradition played its part in the choice that Jesus made.

But we can step back from the setting of the Passover and ask the more general question: What did bread and wine mean at the time of Jesus—in his culture and, for that matter, in other cultures? In the countryside of Galilee, where Jesus grew up, bread obviously stood for survival. It was the staff of life. Without bread people would starve to death. You needed bread on your table to survive and live another day. And wine? Wine, if you could get it, stood for celebration, for having a party. Every now and then in rural Galilee they enjoyed a feast, and people would drink wine in celebration.

Both then and now we all need to survive *and* to celebrate. There is little point in mere survival, in merely getting through life in a grim kind of way, with all the joy of celebration gone out of our existence. Yet there is little point either in an empty celebration that lacks the strength to live as we ought to live. We need to celebrate with strength and survive with joy.

By taking and consecrating bread and wine, Jesus made it possible for us to celebrate with strength and survive with joy. What that bread and wine became in his hands enables us every day to survive and celebrate. What he did with that bread and wine lets us survive with strength and celebrate with joy. His flesh became our real food of strength and his blood our real drink of joy. It is the body and blood of Christ that constitute the true bread of life and the true wine of celebration.

I was grateful for the chance of staying a few days at Pluscarden Abbey. The monks rise early to pray, sing the divine office six times during the day, eat very simple food, and altogether live a throughly austere life. They are also obviously united in a devout and happy community. When you join them for the Eucharist, lift your eyes over the altar to the great window at the east end of the chapel and glimpse the secret at the heart of those monks' existence. You will see, in gleaming red and gold, Christ holding bread and wine. He is the One who enables the monks and all of us to celebrate with strength and survive with joy.

14

The Transfiguration of Jesus (Mark 9:2–8)

Mark, along with the other two Gospel writers, clearly intends to juxtapose the transfiguration and crucifixion of Jesus. The two episodes are held together by five themes, even if they involve sharp contrasts and ironical tensions.

First, two great figures from the Old Testament, Moses and Elijah, join Jesus in the glory of the transfiguration. In the crucifixion, Jesus dies in the company of two unnamed persons, the bandits crucified, respectively, on his right hand and his left. In glory and then in ignominy, he is accompanied by two figures.

Second, Mark notes how in the transfiguration the clothes of Jesus became "dazzling white," with a brilliance that went beyond anything that merely human bleach could ever effect. The clothes of Jesus shared and showed something of his glorious beauty. At Calvary he was stripped of his clothes before being crucified in ugly, humiliating nakedness.

Third, at the transfiguration the voice of the invisible God the Father affirms the identity of Jesus: "This is my Son, the beloved." On Calvary the Roman centurion, who has been in charge of the execution of Jesus, confesses the identity of the man he has just put to death: "Indeed, this man was the Son of God."

Fourth, the two episodes provoke awe and even terror. On the mountain of the transfiguration, Peter, James, and John are "terrified" (Mark 9:6). On Calvary, the manner of Jesus' death left the centurion in awe at the manifestation of the divine (Mark 15:37–39).

Fifth, some followers of Jesus witness both the transfiguration and the crucifixion. Peter, James, and John, the trio who make an inner, intimate group within the Twelve, are with Jesus on the mountain when he is transfigured before their eyes. On Calvary some faithful women look on from a distance, among them Mary Magdalene, Salome, and Mary the mother of James the younger and Joses.

Mark wishes to juxtapose the transfiguration and the crucifixion. Those who read his Gospel quickly may be content to link the two events simply on the basis of Elijah being mentioned in both (Mark 9:4; Mark15:35–36). However, the links prove to be more complex, fascinating, and enriching.

The evangelist holds the transfiguration and crucifixion together because he recognizes how the suffering and glory of Christ are integrated. The Jesus who dies on the cross is the Jesus who was transfigured and who will be transfigured in glory.

15

Bartimaeus Follows Jesus on the Way

Significant words in the English language can be misused in various kinds of ways. One way of misusing words involves applying them without precise respect for their exact meaning. To give an example: every now and then people use, the word "unique" to mean simply important or valuable. They forget the precise meaning of "unique": namely the only case of its kind, the one example of its kind. There are stories in the Gospels to which "unique" genuinely applies: for instance, the healing of Bartimaeus in Mark 10:46–52. This story is unique because it is the only case of its kind in the Gospel according to Mark. Why do I say that?

In this Gospel, Jesus heals many people and even brings one dead person back to life. However, the case of Bartimaeus is unique. He is the only instance of someone healed by Jesus who then becomes his follower. Bartimaeus regains his sight and "follows Jesus on the way." No one else in Mark's Gospel does that. Many others are healed by Jesus. Presumably they do all kinds of good things after being healed. But we do not read of any of these people becoming followers of Jesus, let alone deciding there and then to become a disciple and take to the road with Jesus, as Bartimaeus did.

Bartimaeus regained his sight, his physical sight. But he was also transformed in his spiritual sight. He had cried out to the Lord: "Jesus, Son of David, have mercy on me." He already knew Jesus and already had some kind of faith in him. But now Bartimaeus came spiritually to see Jesus in an even fuller and more generous way. He saw Jesus as the Lord whom he wanted to follow as a disciple. Bartimaeus was blessed in a double way: he regained his sight, and he received the grace to see Jesus as Someone with whom he could throw in his lot, Someone on whom he could stake his life, now and forever. Once blessed again with his physical sight, Bartimaeus immediately followed Jesus on the way. Bartimaeus had lost his sight; he had it back again. But now he was ready to follow Jesus and lose something more than his sight. He was ready to risk losing his life, *with* Jesus and *for* Jesus.

Yes, it *is* a unique case, that healing of Bartimaeus. And do not let us miss where it took place, and where his healing led Bartimaeus. He regained his sight by the roadside in Jericho, and he began to follow Jesus on the way leading up to Jerusalem, the place where Jesus would soon be put to death and raised from the dead. In other words, Bartimaeus joins Jesus on the way of the cross, on the road to Calvary.

In his Gospel, St. Mark was in effect saying to his readers through the case of the blind beggar Bartimaeus: "If you are going to follow Jesus on the way of the cross, you too must have your eyes opened. The Lord must give you real, full spiritual sight if you are to become fully committed and faithful disciples and follow your Master to the place of crucifixion and resurrection." Mark wrote his Gospel at a time of severe persecution, right when Peter, Paul, and others were martyred. Mark had his message for a persecuted Church, but he has his message also for us. If we are going to follow Jesus on the way of the cross, we too must have our eyes opened and our hearts changed. We too must pray, and pray over and over again: "Jesus, Son of David, have mercy on us."

In a sense, whether we like it or not, we all find ourselves on the road from Jericho to Jerusalem. As individuals and as a community, we can be confused and bewildered and pained by many things: by sufferings in our own family; by painful crises in the Church; by problems at our place of work; by awful sufferings in the wider world. On our road from Jericho to Jerusalem, there are many, different things that can afflict us. We cannot escape the cross. Being human beings, as well as being Christians, means finding ourselves on the way of the cross. The big question is always: what are we going to do about the particular crosses that life brings us—as individuals, as families, or as communities? We can react in very different ways. We can get angry and bitter, or cynical and sarcastic. We can become resigned and apathetic. Or we can become like Bartimaeus.

He suffered from his own awful cross: his blindness. He begged the Lord for help: "Jesus, Son of David, have mercy on me." That prayer, which came right from the heart, was heard, and he was cured of his blindness. But his eyes, his spiritual eyes, were also fully opened, and he took the biggest plunge of his life: he decided there and then to follow Jesus on the road of the cross.

Bartimaeus's day began with him as a blind beggar on the roadside at Jericho. His day ended with him walking along behind Jesus on the road to Jerusalem, the road to Calvary. What Bartimaeus did was to put into practice some words of Jesus. He may never have heard those words for himself. But he certainly put them into practice. I'm thinking of the words: "Those who want to save their life will lose it; but those who lose their life for my sake will save it."

Some years ago, an acquaintance of mine was going through a difficult time. He had much to suffer and he was feeling pretty depressed about his faith and his life. One afternoon, during that period of crisis, he switched on the television and began watching someone winning a tennis championship final at Wimbledon. Then he turned away from the television set and remarked: "Christianity is for losers. Success is for tennis players."

At the time I had no answer to give him. It was only later that I thought: "He's wrong about Christianity. Christian faith is *not* for losers; it's for those who are *not afraid* to be losers. Jesus was no loser; and he didn't want his followers to be losers. But Jesus wasn't afraid of being a loser, and he wanted his followers to be like that—people who accept the way of the cross, suffering, and even death, because they are *not afraid* to be losers. Christian faith is for those who, with Jesus and for Jesus, are not afraid to be losers. They know that losing, with Jesus and for Jesus, they will find everything. That's the remarkable thing about Jesus and what he offers: losing is finding.

Going back to Bartimaeus, when he regained his sight, he might have decided to play it safe. He might have decided to head home to some relatives or friends and take good care of himself. He might have joined those who want to save, protect, and safeguard their lives at all costs. Instead, he took to the road with Jesus and headed up to Jerusalem. There and then, he was ready to give everything and even lose his life with Jesus.

What happened to Bartimaeus after he took to the road with Jesus? Where did the way of the cross lead him? We cannot be sure. But one plausible guess made by some scholars is that Bartimaeus finished up in the Christian community and that, over and over again, he told the story of his being cured by Jesus on the roadside at Jericho. Down the years, Bartimaeus repeatedly witnessed to something Jesus had done to him. People would have asked him: "After you were cured, what did you do then?" Bartimaeus would have answered: "I took to the road with Jesus and followed him up to Jerusalem." Whatever happened to Bartimaeus after he met Jesus at Jericho, it all began wonderfully. He was not going to let Jesus out of his sight, and at once he followed him on the way of the cross.

We can and should all be like Bartimaeus: crying out repeatedly, "Jesus, Son of David, have mercy on me," and following Jesus on our way of the cross. In fact, very many of us do just that on Good Friday, when we venerate the cross. We move up to the cross and kiss the feet of the crucified Jesus. We bring up to him all the sufferings that we meet on our road from Jericho to Jerusalem; we lay those sufferings down before Jesus on his cross; and we know that losing our lives, with the crucified Jesus and for the crucified Jesus, means finding—finding the fullness of life, now and forever. Whatever the things, maybe terrible things, we have to suffer, we trust and know that Jesus will hear our prayer: "Jesus, Son of David, have mercy on us." Jesus will hear our prayer, and we can, we must, always follow him.

16

A Scandalous Life and Death

What do the life and crucifixion of Jesus say about our world and its values? His death on a cross exposes the world for what it is. What can we make of a world in which hatred could blaze up in the way it did against the love of God come among us in person? The world had become senseless and deluded through sin. It met the love of God in person by unleashing a storm of hatred that wiped Jesus out.

What does the death of Jesus on the cross say about the "normal" standards of society? These standards embody five key goals: to seek power, go after wealth, avoid pain, achieve success, and cherish being beautiful. Weakness and pain are out. It seems a disgrace to be poor. Failure is unacceptable; you must be successful. You may not look ugly or anything less than beautiful or at least handsome. On the cross Jesus says no to all that. He is powerless and poor, with nothing left to him than a body that endures atrocious physical pain. He seems an ultimate case of failure, dying being two bandits and writhing in ugly agony. His death on Calvary matched some words about the Suffering Servant: "...he had no form or majesty that we should look at him, nothing in his appearance that we should desire him" (Isa 53:2).

The death of Jesus, like his life, comes across as a strange scandal. He was born in a minor corner of the world. His public ministry enjoyed some initial success, but many misunderstood him. Even the core group of disciples, whom he gathered around him and carefully trained, did not understand what he aimed to do. Apart from a few women, at the end they fled and left him to die alone.

We could never say that he lived up front on the world's stage. He passed by everything that seems to give life meaning: financial success, raising a family, travel to exotic places. He did not become a famous writer like some of his Roman contemporaries; he was no political leader. Basically he lived and died alone, with nothing apparently to show for his many "hidden" years and the final, few years of preaching.

What does Christ ultimately teach us through his life and crucifixion? It all comes down to a very simple message: in God's will is our peace. God's love and God's will are all that ultimately matter. That was the way Jesus lived; he did the only thing that finally counts.

At the end Jesus could pass peacefully from this world into the darkness of death because he was going home. His last words according to Luke sum that up: "Father, into your hands I commend my spirit" (Luke 23:46). In another Gospel, Jesus cried out at the end: "It is accomplished" (John 19:30). He had done the one thing that matters. He had loved the God whom he called "Abba," and he had loved all those men and women whom he had met on life's journey.

Part Three

THE SUFFERING AND DEATH OF JESUS

1

The Passion of Jesus
According to Mark

As the passion story according to Mark begins, Jesus comes to the Garden of Gethsemane apparently resigned to what is going to happen to him. If not tranquil, at least he is in charge of the situation. He speaks first to the group of disciples who have accompanied him from the Last Supper, and then he speaks to Peter, James, and John. Finally, he goes off by himself and speaks to God.

As soon as Jesus approaches prayer, he is hit by agony. He becomes "greatly distressed" and "deeply troubled." He is so "gripped by sorrow" that he feels that these emotions could kill him (Mark 14:33–34). Nowhere else do any of the Gospels picture Jesus as being so disoriented and in the grip of such violent emotions.

Earlier in Mark's Gospel, Jesus has challenged James and John: "Are you able to drink the cup that I drink…?" When they reply, "We are able to do so," Jesus has no hesitation in recognizing at once that they will be given the necessary courage: "The cup that I drink you will drink…" (Mark 10:38–39). But now in Gethsemane Jesus prays: "Abba, Father, for you all things are possible; remove this cup from me…." His resolution seems weakened and he does not want to drink his own cup of suffering. Nevertheless, Jesus adds at once: "…yet not what I want but what you want" (Mark 14:36).

In lonely agony, Jesus continues to struggle right through his long prayer to God. Obviously the imminent threat of violent death causes Jesus to be distraught and troubled. When finally facing his terrible fate on the cross, he does not behave with composure, let alone act with stoic endurance. In these last hours before his arrest, Jesus loses his nerve and looks for an escape route. Yet he ends his terrified prayer by reaffirming his obedience to the divine will. He can only push on, believing that his Father wishes him to do so. Some words from *Markings* by Dag Hammarskjöld catch the Gethsemane experience: "Only one feat is possible—not to have run away."

Right before the agony in Gethsemane, Mark has indicated a second reason for the terrible distress of Jesus. After gathering a core group of disciples, he has instructed and protected them until this moment. Now he watches helplessly as they break up. Judas has already gone away into the night and will guide a paramilitary group to arrest Jesus. All the others will desert Jesus as soon as his enemies arrive. Peter will swear on oath that he does not even know his Master.

Jesus has just warned all of them that they will abandon him and Peter that he will deny him (Mark 14:26–31). However, the warning makes no difference. The cowardice of these male disciples leaves Jesus to suffer his passion and death isolated and undefended.

Once Jesus is arrested, a whole series of scenes follow with breathless speed. He is confronted by various individuals and groups: the high priest, Caiaphas, at the head of the Jewish council; the Roman prefect, Pontius Pilate, who questions him; the crowd who cry out for Jesus to be crucified; the soldiers who scourge, mock, and hustle him off to crucifixion and death on Calvary.

In all these chaotic scenes no one spoke up for Jesus, let alone did anything for him. Here Mark differs from Matthew and Luke. Matthew tells of a painful dream that prompted Pilate's wife to take Jesus' part and urge her husband not to act against "that innocent man." Luke mentions the women who wept for Jesus on the way of the cross, as well as the criminal who was crucified with Jesus and spoke up for him: "...this man has done nothing wrong."

In Mark's story no one took Jesus' side. The only "exception" was Simon of Cyrene, who was forced by the Roman soldiers to carry the cross. The scourging had left Jesus in such a weakened state that he might not have made it alive to Calvary. Right through to the end, Jesus was left alone and undefended.

It is not until Jesus dies that anyone takes his side. Of all people, the Roman centurion who has been in charge of the execution squad breaks through to the truth and says: "Indeed, this man was the Son of God." It is only then that we learn that many women among the followers of Jesus have been courageously and faithfully present at his death (Mark 15:39–41).

The bleak and painful scenes in Mark's passion story invite us to imaginatively add ourselves to the action as an "extra." In our prayer we might join the holy women in supplying what Peter and the male disciples failed to give: some support to Jesus in the terrible death he suffered for us.

2

The Passion and Death of Jesus

There always seems something strange and even senseless about the death of any human being. This is especially so in the case of Jesus. It is the mystery of mysteries that he who was Life itself suffered the experience of death. How could we even begin to understand that? It seems absurd to think of Jesus undergoing death.

If it is hard for us to tackle this mystery, which was true also for the first Christians. In the passion stories they wrote, the evangelists attempted to respond to the challenge of making some sense of the horror of Jesus' passion and death. They knew that they could do so only by writing at length. John devoted two chapters to the passion of Jesus; those chapters are much longer than the two chapters that he devoted to the resurrection narratives. Mark spent two chapters on the passion story—something quite out of proportion to his very brief treatment of the resurrection.

All four evangelists point us to the conclusion that is summed up by the Second Eucharistic Prayer when it says about Jesus, "Before he was given up to death, a death he freely accepted." By doing so, Jesus humanized, so to speak, the absurd horror of his crucifixion. He accepted his mission, among us and for us, right through to its ultimate consequences. Jesus showed us how accepting suffering can prove healing and life-giving. In his unique case, such acceptance proved healing and life-giving for the whole world.

It is not, of course, easy to endorse this conclusion for ourselves. It proves remorselessly difficult for us to accept suffering, especially in situations that seem senseless or in painful situations that we ourselves have caused. In a kind of silent revolt against God, we can resist accepting suffering for a long time. What Jesus in his passion shows us is that, unless we consciously and freely accept them, our sufferings will have no real meaning. They will begin to have proper meaning once we accept them. If we accept them, we will be liberated from the power of evil, and our accepted sufferings can help cleanse and set right a damaged world. As Jesus shows, accepted suffering can be the highest form of transforming love.

When he was dying, Jesus was taunted by his enemies: "He saved others; he cannot save himself. Let the Christ, the King of Israel, come down now from the cross, that we may *see and believe*" (Mark 15:31–32 [italics mine]). But Jesus stayed on the cross with his fellow sufferers, and he died with them. Yet very soon the centurion and vast multitude of others did "see and believe."

The dying cry of Jesus had reached through to the soldier's heart. When Mark wrote, "…uttering a loud cry, Jesus gave up his spirit (*exepneusen*)," (15:37), that was no ordinary way of talking about death, no ordinary Greek word for dying. Jesus died actively; his death and dying cry had an immediate effect. They went to the heart of one man, the Roman centurion. He was there to do his duty, as a soldier who could not always keep his hands clean and even on occasions had to put innocent people to death. It was such a person who became the first human being in Mark's Gospel to break through the divine incognito and recognize Jesus for who he was: "Indeed this man was the Son of God" (15:39).

***

Jesus was not there to save us from suffering, but to give meaning to suffering.

He did not attempt to deny that suffering pervades our existence. He did not dream of some utopia that would bring freedom from suffering in this world. Nor did he rebel in anger against suffering. He knew that suffering is a sacrament where we meet God.

Baptism and all the other sacraments do not work without a word. Likewise, suffering and death remain senseless, as long as they remain without a positive word that gives them some meaning, even some mysterious meaning. The tragedy is not that we suffer, but that we can waste suffering, treat it as an awkward nuisance or a dreadful affliction to be avoided at all costs.

How should we think about our own suffering and death? If we do not find reflection on personal suffering to be easy, we can be encouraged by St. Paul. He found it hard to think about his suffering and threatening death. That is the wonderful drama of his Second Letter to the Corinthians. Over and over again he came back to the theme of suffering in that letter. Apparently it took Paul a considerable amount of time to recognize that his worst sufferings were not merely a terrible obstacle to the work that he wanted to do for Jesus. He accepted the sufferings that came to him in his ministry, only because the Lord spoke to him: "My grace is sufficient for you, for power is made perfect in weakness" (2 Cor 12:9). Like Paul, we need a word from Jesus to show us some meaning in suffering and join the apostle in saying: "When I am weak, then I am strong" (2 Cor 12:10).

Modern advertising prompts us to think of the young, the strong, the beautiful and the successful. Yes, Jesus was young. But he died like someone incredibly weak, with no one to defend him. After the scourging, when he hung dying on the cross, he looked ugly, dreadfully ugly. He had suffered atrociously and seemed like one of the great losers of all time. But God took this weak, powerless "failure" to be the means of our redemption.

Some years ago I was in Florence to hear a conference by the Irish president, Mary McAleese, who spoke at a center of a world community for Christian meditation. Her lecture was splendid and so too were the questions and comments. I can never forget what the Lutheran pastor of Florence said: "We have followed too long a powerful God; we need a weak God." On Good Friday our powerful God died in weakness; the Gospels narrate the death of the "weak" Son of God.

Each Good Friday, through the Veneration of the Cross, we think with Jesus about our own suffering and death and lay our sufferings at his crucified feet. May that gesture bring us to accept what we endure and then find in our sufferings the healing and peace that we all need.

3

The Passion of Jesus According to Matthew and Luke

Among the challenging themes that color Matthew's passion narrative, one should recall how different characters try to shake off their responsibility for what is happening to Jesus. To begin with, Judas brings back the thirty pieces of silver and tries to return the money to the chief priests and elders. "I have sinned," he says. "I have brought an innocent man to his death." But the religious authorities will not accept the money from him. So he throws the money not into any of the courts of the Temple where all the faithful would attend, but into the sanctuary, to which only priests, the guardians of the sanctuary, have access. Then he hurries off to hang himself.

The priests, in a way, try to shake off their responsibility. They refuse to put the "blood money" back in the treasury of the Temple. They use it to buy a field to serve as a burial place for foreigners.

After Pilate comes to sit in judgment on Jesus, he is warned by his wife to "have nothing to do with that innocent man." The Roman prefect then tries to extricate himself from being involved in Jesus' fate by taking water and washing his hands in full view of the crowd.

When we see these leading people in Matthew's passion narrative trying to disown their responsibility, we can only ask:

Who then is responsible for the death of Jesus? We can hardly read the story without feeling a haunting sense of the common responsibility we share with Judas, the chief priests, and Pilate. These figures represent all of humanity. Judas represents the followers of Jesus; the chief priests represent the Jews who do not believe in Jesus; and Pilate represents the rest of humanity. Two individuals and a group stand in for all of us. The sins of treachery and expediency that lead them to collaborate in sending Jesus to his death belong to us all. We all played a part in the execution of Jesus. But it is hard to accept that it was and is our responsibility. A wonderful old lady, who spent nearly all her life in top circles, at Harvard University, in the foreign service, and then in Washington, sadly summed up for me the common reluctance to admit guilt: "All that so many say is, 'Mistakes were made but not by me.'"

Gazing at Jesus on the cross, we can only say: "I played my part in that. Lord, have mercy on me, and remember me when you come into your kingdom."

In Luke's passion narrative, healing and forgiving provide a theme that runs right through the story. This is hardly surprising. From the very start of his Gospel, Luke has highlighted the work of salvation. Two majestic prayers enunciate this theme: the "Benedictus" glorifies God for "salvation from our enemies and from the hand of all who hate us," while the "Magnificat" praises "God, my Savior" (Luke 1:47, 71). When Jesus is born, an angel of the Lord announces to the shepherds "good news of great joy...to you is born this day in the city of David a Savior..." (Luke 2:10–11). Throughout his ministry, Jesus is bent on healing, forgiving, and saving people. Luke shows us how Jesus continues to do so, even as he moves into the passion.

In the Garden of Gethsemane, Jesus makes a last effort to heal and save Judas. He acknowledges the traitor personally and speaks to him by name: "Judas, would you betray the Son of man with a kiss?" It is only in Luke's Gospel that we find Jesus, at the very moment of betrayal and arrest, acknowledging Judas by his name. It is a final, fruitless effort to change and heal the heart of the traitor.

At once one of the disciples (Peter, as we know from John's Gospel) draws a sword, strikes at those who have come to arrest Jesus, and succeeds in cutting off the right ear of a servant of the high priest. Jesus says, "Enough of that," touches the ear of the wounded man, and heals him. The other Gospel writers all mention the scuffle in which the servant loses his ear. Only Luke reports this act of healing. It is the first of several acts of healing and forgiveness that occur before Jesus dies on Calvary.

It is only in Luke's passion story that Jesus turns and looks at Peter after Peter has denied him. That look makes Peter remember the Lord's warning: "...before the cock crows today you will deny me three times." Peter slips away and begins to weep bitterly. Through his reproachful but healing glance, Jesus has helped Peter to repent and be forgiven.

In Luke's passion narrative Jesus also does something for two unlikely characters: Herod Antipas and Pontius Pilate. After Jesus is arrested, Pilate learns that he is a Galilean and sends him off to the ruler of Galilee. It is only in Luke's Gospel that we read about Jesus being brought before Herod. There follows an ugly scene in which Jesus is mocked, treated with contempt, and then sent back to Pilate. Rather surprisingly, Luke adds: "That same day Herod and Pilate became friends with each other; before this they had been enemies." In his healing and saving work, Jesus does something even for two dismal persons: a ruthless Roman prefect and a corrupt minor king.

When the crucifixion takes place, Luke tells us of Jesus praying for those who are putting him to death: "Father, forgive them, for they know not what they are doing." When one of the criminals turns to Jesus in prayer, Jesus promises him final salvation: "This day, you will be with me in paradise."

From the beginning to the end of Luke's passion story, Jesus reaches out to heal, forgive, and save people, even those who have deserted him. When Jesus dies, Luke tells us: "*all his friends* and the women who had followed him from Galilee stood at a distance and saw these things." From the other Gospel writers we learn of the women who had stayed faithfully with Jesus to the very end. Only Luke enlarges the group of those who were courageously present at the crucifixion to include the male disciples. In a generous way, worthy of Jesus himself, the evangelist anticipates the healing and forgiveness that will come to the male disciples after the resurrection.

4

Holy Thursday
According to John

Ten years ago in Philadelphia I entered a sacristy to prepare for
a funeral Mass. Above the vestments laid out on the table was a
sign that gave this advice: "Priest of God, celebrate this Mass as
if it were your first Mass, your last Mass, your only Mass." It
struck me how this advice applied above all to Jesus, the great
High Priest. On the first Holy Thursday, along with what was to
follow on Good Friday, Holy Saturday, and Easter Sunday, Jesus
celebrated his first Mass, his last Mass, and his only Mass.

The passage from John 13:1–15 that is read at the Eucharist
on Holy Thursday sets the story of that first, last, and only Mass
in the broadest context: the context of divine greatness and
human service. The Gospel puts together two relationships that
constituted the existence of Jesus: one vertical toward his
Father and the other horizontal toward us. We read of a vertical relationship of divine greatness and a horizontal relationship of human service.

The Gospel passage begins with the divine greatness and a
vertical relationship: "...Jesus knew that the hour had come for
him to pass from this world to the Father....Jesus knew that the
Father had put all things into his hands, and that he had come
from God and was going to God." Jesus had come *from* God and
was returning *to* God. For Jesus, God was the beginning and the
end. Everything in between was a parenthesis. Everything
between that coming and that returning had meaning only

insofar as it came from that beginning and related forward to that end. For Jesus, everything between his coming and his going referred *back* to God and *forward* to God.

There is amazing and profound simplicity in the way this Gospel reading opens. Time is running out fast. The hour has come for Jesus to pass from this world to the Father and to his final glory with the Father. This is the scene of divine greatness that the Gospel of John puts before us on Holy Thursday evening. What overshadows everything is the relationship between Jesus and his Father, between Jesus and the Father who has put all power and authority into his hands.

Then the Gospel sets that scene of divine greatness along-side a story of utterly simple, human service. Jesus gets up from the table and begins to wash the feet of his disciples. "All things" are in his hands, and now he takes into those hands their feet to wash them and dry them. Before he passes from this world to the Father, Jesus performs this humble act of service.

Jesus tells Peter: "At this moment you do not know what I am doing. But later you will understand." Yet one might ask: At least in this life, would Peter ever fully understand what was happening then? Will any of us ever fully understand the two sides of this wonderful scene: Jesus going home to God and Jesus kneeling to wash and dry his disciples' feet? Which is the harder thing to understand? His divine greatness, as he comes from God and goes back to God? Or his humble act of human service, as he kneels with a basin and towel at the feet of his disciples?

Ultimately we face here an extraordinary mystery, the mystery of Jesus who was at home with God but whose love drove him to serve us and give himself up for us all. On Holy Thursday we remember with love and gratitude the first, last, and only Mass at which Jesus instituted the Eucharist. John's Gospel encourages us to recall how divine greatness and hum-ble, human service surrounded the institution of the Eucharist.

5

Judas Iscariot

Judas and his treachery obviously affected all four Gospel writers deeply. To appreciate what they felt, we can look at them in turn.

Mark, who would be followed in this by Matthew and Luke, tells us that Judas betrayed his master with a kiss (Mark 14:45). Nowhere else in the Gospels do we find Jesus and his disciples exchanging a kiss. Nor is anyone else recalled as having kissed Jesus or been kissed by him. Jesus takes children into his arms and presumably kisses them. But we are never precisely told that he does so. Only Judas exchanges a kiss with Jesus.

Then Luke, writing a little later than Mark, adds that "Satan entered into Judas." When Judas went off to discuss with the chief priests some convenient way of betraying Jesus, he was doing diabolic work (Luke 22:3–4). Attentive readers will recall that, after tempting Jesus, the devil "left him until an opportune time" (Luke 4:13). Now, through Judas Iscariot, such an opportune time has come up for Satan—the hour of "the power of darkness" (Luke 22:53).

In reporting what happened in Gethsemane, Luke tells, however, of a final effort by Jesus to save Judas. Jesus acknowledges Judas personally—even by name: "Judas, would you betray the Son of man with a kiss?" (Luke 22:48). It is only in this Gospel that Jesus acknowledges Judas by name at the moment of betrayal and arrest. This is the initial example of Jesus setting himself, right through the passion account of Luke, to heal and save people.

Thus Luke speaks of Judas doing diabolic work and being under the power of Satan. However, he modifies a bit that grim picture by presenting Jesus as appealing very personally to Judas at the actual moment of being arrested.

Matthew's portrayal of Judas proves somewhat bleaker. He dramatizes Judas's wickedness by having him ask the chief priests for money: "What will you give me if I hand him over to you?" (Matt 26:15). In two other Gospels the priests take the initiative by offering Judas some unspecified amount of money (Mark 14:11; Luke 22:5–6). But in Matthew's Gospel it is Judas who not only asks for money but is also given some money in advance, thirty pieces of silver.

According to all four Gospels, Jesus foretells at the Last Supper the treachery of Judas (Mark 14:18–21; Luke 22:21–23; John 13:21–30). Matthew adds a special, little touch. When Jesus announces sadly, "...one of you will betray me," the disciples are very upset by this announcement. They begin to ask one after another: "Is it I, *Lord*." Finally, Judas puts the question to Jesus: "Is it I, *Rabbi*?" (Matt 26:20–25 [italics mine]). He does not call Jesus "Lord" but merely "Rabbi." He uses a public title or form of address when he speaks to Jesus. Judas is already outside the circle of those who honor and love Jesus as their Lord.

Lastly, we can look at Judas in the fourth Gospel. John prepares readers well beforehand for Judas's treachery—long before he writes those chilling words: "The devil put it into the heart of Judas, son of Simon Iscariot, to betray Jesus" (John 13:2). Way back at the end of the discourse on the Bread of Life, Peter speaks to Jesus and makes a magnificent confession on behalf of the core group of disciples: "Lord, to whom shall we go? You have the words of eternal life. We have come to believe and know that you are the Holy One of God" (John 6:69). Yet Jesus responds sadly: "Did I not choose you, the Twelve, and one of you is a devil?" The Gospel writer explains at once: "He was speaking of Judas, son of Simon Iscariot, since this was the man, one of the Twelve, who was to betray him" (John 6:70–71). Like Luke, John tells us that Judas did the devil's work, but he says this many chapters earlier.

Then, when describing a dinner Lazarus and his two sisters held for Jesus, John has something further to say about Judas's bad character. He merely pretends to care for the poor. In objecting to the extravagant gesture of honor and love Mary shows to Jesus, his real motive is that the money she has paid for the perfume (the equivalent of almost a year's wages for a laborer) could have gone into the common funds. Judas, who keeps the purse, might have helped himself to even more money. He is "a thief," who has no commitment to the poor and is incapable of appreciating Mary's lavish gesture of love (John 12:1–6).

Yes, it is at the Last Supper that the devil puts it into the heart of Judas to betray Jesus. But, as the fourth Gospel shows, Judas's sinful life has prepared the way for a supreme act of treachery.

6
Judas, Jesus, and Peter

The Gospel of John introduces, from the beginning, many images that prepare the way for the supreme act of love enacted in the suffering and death of Jesus. This happens, for instance, through the elaborate account of Jesus as the good shepherd who gives his own life for his sheep (John 10:1–18).

Various elements combine to fill out the picture: for instance, the gate to the sheepfold used by the true shepherd when he comes to call his flock. There are also thieves and bandits who do not enter that way; they climb in "by another way." Then, unlike the good shepherd, hired hands run away and abandon the sheep if they spot the approach of wolves. The passage on the good shepherd throws light on what comes a few chapters later: a detachment of soldiers and police arrests Jesus, and Peter quickly denies his Lord (John 18:1–18).

The scene of Jesus' arrest, an enclosed garden, evokes another walled zone, the sheepfold of chapter 10 of the Gospel of John. We have been told that Judas is "a thief" (John 12:6). Now, not only like a thief who intends to "steal" but also like a bandit intending to "kill and destroy," he approaches Jesus, the one who has "come" that all "might have life, and have it abundantly"(John 10:10). Judas turns up under cover of darkness, the time when thieves and wolves strike.

When the soldiers and police arrive, Jesus, like the good shepherd, will not run away but stands his ground. He surrenders himself and protects his sheep: "if you are looking for me, let these others go" (John 18:8). These words evoke the whole meaning of Jesus' passion: it took place—to echo the Creed—"for us and for our salvation." The others go free, but Jesus allows himself to be arrested and to be put to death for all others and for their everlasting benefit.

Right there and then in the garden, "these others" include Peter. He proceeds to act like one of the "hired hands," whose defection in the hour of danger highlights the steady commitment of the good shepherd.

Unlike Jesus who tells the truth about himself (John 18:5, 8), Peter denies the truth about himself (John 18:17, 25). Where Jesus says "I am," Peter insists "I am not." The story sets denials that come from Peter (John 18:15–27) over against Jesus' truthful replies to the high priest (John 18:15–27). Jesus witnesses to his mission (John 18:20) while Peter repeatedly denies being his disciple.

Right through the passion narrative, Jesus behaves with serene self-control; he remains in charge of what happens (e.g., John 18:4; 19:11). It is in an uncontrolled fashion that Peter faces the situation of Jesus' arrest and the unfolding events of the passion. He strikes out wildly at the servant of the high priest (John 18:10). Then he lacks the courage to admit being a follower of Jesus and being with him in the garden just a few hours earlier.

During the Last Supper Peter has protested that he will follow Jesus to the end and even lay down his life for him (John 13:37). But when "the thieves, bandits, and wolves" arrive, Peter behaves like a hired hand. It will take the death and resurrection of Jesus to transform Peter into a true shepherd, ready to lay down his life for his Master's flock (John 21:18–19).

7

The Veil of Veronica

Around the world one of the most successful exhibitions during the Jubilee Year 2000 was *Seeing Salvation* in the National Gallery, London. Centered on the death of Christ, it reminded its visitors forcefully of the "veil" of "Veronica" ("true likeness"), an image of Christ's face found everywhere in medieval Europe.

A woman who was not a follower of Jesus supposedly saw him on the way to Calvary, took pity on him, and wiped the sweat from his face with a cloth. As a reward for her compassion, his features were miraculously transferred to the cloth. One old tradition identified her with the woman whom Jesus cured of a chronic hemorrhage (Mark 5:25–34). Some placed her among the group of holy women who followed Jesus to the crucifixion and wept over his tragic fate (Luke 23:27–31). Her name, "Veronica," belonged to the legend of a true likeness of Jesus' face left on her cloth when she wiped his face.

The story of the image on the cloth evoked not only the passion of Jesus but also his presence in the Eucharist, which he instituted on the night before he died. In many medieval prayer books the scene of Veronica holding the cloth accompanied prayers to be said at Mass when the Host was elevated after the words of institution.

As various items in the exhibition *Seeing Salvation* illustrated, sometimes Veronica was depicted holding the cloth that carried an image of the suffering Christ; sometimes angels held it; and sometimes the image stood by itself. In an engraving by

Albrecht Dürer exhibited at *Seeing Salvation*, Veronica does not appear. Christ stares out from under a crown of thorns with a pained expression as blood trickles down from his forehead. The two angels who hold the image respond to the scene with expressions of extreme grief on their faces. They invite an intense emotional response from the viewers. The features of Christ's face in this engraving made by Dürer in 1513 resemble those of the artist himself. It seems that Dürer identified himself with Jesus and wanted to join Jesus in his suffering—a vivid, artistic example of "compassion" or suffering with the Lord on his way to death by crucifixion.

By the time of Dürer, devotion to the "Holy Face," then no longer necessarily connected with the legend of Veronica, permeated all levels of society. Images of the suffering face of Christ were widely available. Some versions pictured Christ with a crown of thorns, others did not. In some versions his eyes were open, in others closed. Nowadays the face on the Shroud of Turin, with its eyes closed in death, is the most familiar likeness of the suffering Christ.

Paintings or sculptures of Christ nailed to the cross express that love which brought him on mission to save human beings and made him so weak and vulnerable as he followed his mission through to the end. We all have our preferences among the innumerable representations of the crucifixion.

Yet images that pick out his suffering face may focus even more effectively our compassion. As people moved around the exhibition *Seeing Salvation*, various versions of the veil of Veronica reduced them to silence and clearly touched them with a sense of the love that brought Christ to suffer and die for all of us.

8

Holy Saturday

Some have described Holy Saturday as the longest day in human history. Certainly it can seem the longest day in the Church's liturgical year. How might we spend Holy Saturday? What might feed into our prayer on that day? Let me suggest three possibilities.

1. One way to spend Holy Saturday would be to recall imaginatively one person or some people whom we read about in the Gospels and imagine how they might have spent the evening and the day that followed the death of Jesus. We could think of the Jewish high priest Caiaphas or the Roman prefect Pontius Pilate and reflect on what they might have been thinking and saying at home with their family and friends. Matthew's Gospel tells us that Caiaphas and company wanted the tomb of Jesus to be guarded, so as to make sure that nothing "unfortunate" could happen. Pilate made a deployment of soldiers available, those soldiers who were to enter Christian depictions of the resurrection thousands of times. What went through the minds of Caiaphas, Pilate, and the guard during the evening of Good Friday and the long hours of the first Holy Saturday?

Or we might think of Simon of Cyrene, first recalled in Mark's Gospel as being abruptly forced to carry the cross for Jesus and named as "the father of Alexander and Rufus" (Mark 15:21). Many scholars have commented that these three names are mentioned because Simon and his family became followers of Jesus. That apparently chance meeting on the way to Calvary changed Simon forever. Did Simon begin by feeling sharp anger and humiliation at being forced to carry a cross for a condemned criminal? Was he changed even on the way to Calvary or on Calvary itself? Did Simon begin by seeing only the cross and end by seeing only Jesus?

What about other people involved in the story of Jesus' crucifixion? According to Mark 15:39, when the centurion in charge of the execution saw how Jesus died, he declared: "Indeed this man was the Son of God." How then did the centurion spend the first Good Friday evening and Holy Saturday? What was he thinking and what might he have said to other soldiers?

In this way we can call up for ourselves some or all the other people who belong in the passion narrative: Peter, Mary Magdalene, Joseph of Arimathea, Nicodemus, the beloved disciple, the Blessed Virgin Mary, and the other holy women whom the four Gospels mention. We could quietly spend Holy Saturday in their company, sharing in their memories, grief, and prayers.

2. A second and very different way of spending prayerfully Holy Saturday is suggested by the site of Jesus' execution: Golgotha, "the place of a skull" (Mark 15: 22). Jesus was the Lord of life, but the world had closed in on him and brought him to a violent death at "the place of the skull." Pondering the *places* of the passion story could be another way of letting it all fill us with prayer.

At the end of his life Jesus moved away from a reasonably large place, the region of Galilee. He came up to the city of Jerusalem and sent two of his disciples to arrange for a house where they could all celebrate together the Last Supper (Mark 14:13–15). From the house he went into a garden where he was arrested, to be brought first to the palace of Caiaphas and then to Pilate's praetorium. From there he was led to death at "the place of the skull" and finally placed in a tomb.

From the time Jesus left Galilee, everything closed in on him. The places became smaller and smaller: a city, a house, a garden, a palace, a praetorium, the place of a skull, and finally a tomb cut out of rock. The world took Jesus away from the broad space of Galilee to kill him and shut him into a tomb.

But, with his resurrection from the dead, everything will open up again. An angel of the Lord and then Jesus himself tells two holy women that he will rendezvous with his disciples in Galilee (Matt 28:7, 10). There they will meet him and go out into the whole world, knowing that he will be with them across the whole earth and to the very end of time.

The sequence of places—from Galilee to the place of a skull and the tomb and then back to Galilee and out into the wide world—says something valuable about Our Lord's death and resurrection. In death, he endured a terrible closing in and closing down. However, he rose from death to reach out into the whole world. Everywhere and always our world will be charged with his life-giving presence and power.

3. A third way of spending at least part of Holy Saturday in prayer would be to think of some favorite title of Jesus and let it focus our gaze on the cross or on the tomb. Addressing Jesus, we can say:

> You are the Word of God spoken to us, but you ended in the silence of death.
> You are the Lamb of God, and you have taken away the sins of the whole world.
> You are the Bread of Life, broken for us, broken to give us eternal life.
> You are the Light of the world, but you went into the darkness of death.
> You are the Good Shepherd, and you died for your sheep.
> You are the Way, the Way that led you to Calvary.

You are the Truth, denied and ignored by many but
  enlightening our world.
You are the Life that came to death but rose from death.
You are the image of the unseen God, and you became a
  crucified image, our Crucified God.

Part Four

THE RESURRECTION AND RISEN LIFE OF JESUS

1

The Resurrection
According to Matthew

Essentially the four Gospel writers tell the same story when they report the death, burial, and resurrection of Jesus. Yet attentive reading of their texts will catch various details and insights that are special to each of them.

In Easter liturgy for two of the three liturgical years, Mark, Luke, and John have it all over Matthew. From the vigil service on Holy Saturday right through the Easter Octave, Matthew makes only one appearance at Mass—supplying the short Gospel for Easter Monday (Matt 28:8–15). Yet in Matthew's Easter chapter (Matt 28: 1–20), a varied cast of characters, obviously along with the risen Jesus himself, can illuminate our world and give direction to Christian discipleship. There are five sections in that chapter which invite close reading:

1. The coming of two women to the tomb of Jesus
2. The descent of an angel
3. The appearance of the Christ
4. The bribing of the guard
5. The great commission to evangelize the world

Matthew opens his Easter chapter by introducing the theme of light in a way that recalls the start of Jesus' ministry. It is "at the dawning of the first day of the week" (Matt 28:1) that Mary Magdalene and another disciple also called Mary approach the tomb of Jesus. Careful readers will remember that Matthew has used "the dawning of light" to characterize the time when Jesus began to proclaim the kingdom of God: "...the people who sat in darkness have seen a great light; and on those who sat in the region of death, light has dawned" (4:16). The end of Jesus' story more than confirms the beginning. With his resurrection, the light of the divine kingdom has definitively dawned and will never be dimmed. The two women are walking into a day on which the sun will never set.

Mary Magdalene and her companion, just as they had faithfully followed Jesus to Calvary and "looked at" him on the cross (Matt 27:55–56), now want to be near the body of Jesus and "look at" his tomb (Matt 28:1). Instead, they are present when the tomb is dramatically opened, receive from an angel of the Lord the message of Jesus' resurrection, and can witness for themselves that the tomb is now empty (Matt 28:6, 8).

In Matthew's narrative, an earthquake had marked the death of Jesus and opened the tombs of many holy people (Matt 27:51–53). Now a great earthquake works, with the angel who "descends from heaven," to roll away the massive stone blocking the entrance to Jesus' tomb and reveal his resurrection. The angel of the Lord acts with the divine power and authority that overcome death—a theme symbolized by the way he removes the stone and "sits upon" it. The majestic angel is also a kind of stand-in for Jesus; his radiant glory (Matt 28:3) reflects something of the beauty of the risen Jesus himself.

The two women run from the tomb with "fear and great joy" (Matt 28:8). The astonishing news of the resurrection calls for some holy fear as an appropriate human reaction. Yet joy, even "great joy," must have the last word. Once again Matthew's choice of language should prompt the reader into recalling some other persons at the beginning of the Gospel: namely, the wise men from the East, who "rejoiced with very great joy" when their star led them to find the newborn Christ

Child (Matt 2:10). The birth of Jesus and his resurrection from the dead trigger the same overwhelming delight in friends of God—in the wise men at the beginning of the story and in the holy women at the end.

When they are on their way to announce the news of the resurrection to the male disciples, Jesus appears to the "two Marys" (Matt 28:9–10). The holy women have already received the angelic message of the resurrection and have seen the empty tomb for themselves. Now a personal encounter with the risen Jesus himself confirms what they know. Matthew says that "Jesus *met* them" (italics mine). This is the only text in the whole of the New Testament that speaks of Jesus himself "meeting" anybody else; it suggests how highly Jesus values the two women and their mission. Like the wise men with the Christ Child (Matt 2:11), they kneel before Jesus and "worship" him—the appropriate reverence to be paid to Jesus during his earthly life and, even more, after his resurrection.

When Jesus speaks to the two women, he seemingly repeats what the angel has already said to them: "...tell his disciples, '...he is going ahead of you to Galilee; there you will see him'" (Matt 28: 7). However, a lovely change in two words carries a wealth of meaning. Jesus himself tells the women to announce this same message to "my brothers" (Matt 28:10). The disciples of the risen Lord are now even more than "mere" disciples: they are "my brothers and sisters" in the new family of God.

Matthew next inserts a story about the bribing of the soldiers (Matt 28:11–15) who had been posted to watch over the tomb of Jesus. They thought they were guarding a corpse, and then with a dramatic and ironic twist, they were so terrified by the glorious angel of the Lord that they fell down and "became like dead men" (Matt 28:4). While the women are on their way to tell the male disciples of the resurrection, the guards also go into Jerusalem and report to the chief priests "everything that had happened" (Matt 28:11). They then receive a large sum of money to spread the false story that the disciples had come by night and stolen the body of Jesus. Apart from the parable of the talents (Matt 25:18–27), Matthew nowhere mentions money except in connection with Judas and the soldiers who had been at the tomb (Matt 26:14–15, 27:3, 6; 28:12–15). The resurrection of Jesus from the dead prompts a second betrayal for money. Judas had been "bought" to make use of what he knew: namely, where Jesus would be found when the temple police came to arrest him. The soldiers are "bought off" to suppress what they know through the startling intervention of the angel of the Lord at the tomb. Something sadly venial about Judas and the soldiers serves as a negative foil to highlight the sheer grandeur of Jesus' self-sacrificing death, his glorious resurrection from the dead, and the status of the two holy women who become the first witnesses to the resurrection.

The male disciples keep the rendezvous in Galilee and are commissioned to evangelize the world (Matt 28:16–20). The Gospel of Matthew ends by emphasizing the comprehensive authority of the risen Jesus: "*All* authority *in heaven and on earth* has been given to me. Go therefore and make disciples of *all nations*, baptizing them in the name of the Father, and of the Son, and of the Holy Spirit, and teaching them to observe *all* that I have commanded you. And behold I am with you *always*, even to the *end of time*" (italics mine). In this way Matthew concludes his account of the resurrection of Jesus by putting it into a perspective that embraces not only the whole world but also the entire universe ("heaven" as well as "earth") as we might say, all space and all time.

The impact of Christ's resurrection, the evangelist indicates, affects everyone and everything that make up the entire cosmos and its total history. It is no wonder then that he introduces here the rite of baptism in the name of God, now known to be the Father, and the Son, and the Holy Spirit. The tripersonal God, who has created all things and rules all things, is revealed in the new creation, initiated by Christ's resurrection from the dead and disclosed through the life and worship of the baptized faithful.

Most years, from Holy Saturday until the end of the Easter Octave, the Gospels of Mark, Luke, and John take the front row. But Matthew's final chapter also has spiritual treasures that can enlighten our faith in the resurrection of Jesus. If we take time to ponder prayerfully that chapter, it too can enrich our sense of the unique blessings brought by the first Easter.

2

Mark on Darkness and Light

Switching from darkness to light characterizes the way Mark tells the whole story of the death and resurrection of Jesus. It is not simply that he speaks of darkness being over the land for hours at the time of crucifixion (Mark 15:33) and light coming with the resurrection (Mark 16:2). We can track the alternation of darkness and light right through his narrative of the passion and resurrection. Scenes of darkness and light follow one another with dramatic power.

First, the enemies of Jesus plot ways of arresting him "by stealth" and doing away with him (Mark 14:1). In darkness they take steps to end his life. Almost immediately there comes a scene of light and love: a generous, anonymous woman pours precious ointment over the head and shoulders of Jesus (Mark 14:3–9). She makes a beautiful, extravagant gesture of love toward him.

The next scene has Judas slipping away to meet the chief priests and find some way for betraying Jesus. The authorities promise to give him money in return for his dark deed (Mark 14:10–11). At once we move to the light and love that Jesus shows at the Last Supper when instituting the Eucharist (Mark 14:12–25).

The story of the passion takes us into the darkness of the Garden of Gethsemane and all that follows. When Jesus is arrested, all his male followers run away into the night and leave him to face alone his suffering and death.

At the end of Mark's Gospel, light and life return forever. Three women, bound to Jesus with faithful love, go to the tomb of Jesus just after dawn has come (Mark 16:2). Without knowing it, they are walking into the light of a day on which the sun will never set. Through the whole passion and resurrection story of Mark, scenes of darkness and light have alternated. At the end, a light dawns that will never go away. Light and love will remain forever. As an African proverb says, "Where there is love, it is never dark."

3
The Eyes of Love
(John 20:1–9)

Every word and every phrase count in the four Gospels, especially in John. In the Easter story John inserts a rich and telling phrase: Mary Magdalene comes to the tomb of Jesus "while it was still dark." In John's Gospel, darkness represents unbelief and hatred, while light expresses faith and love in the One who is the Light of the world. The evangelist speaks of darkness being still there, early on the first Easter morning. That darkness will last until someone comes to believe in the risen Christ and love him.

Chapter 20 of the Gospel of John tells the beautiful story of Mary Magdalene meeting the risen Christ and in love coming to recognize him as her risen Lord. However, first the chapter focuses on another figure, the beloved disciple.

This mysterious character begins to appear clearly in John's Gospel at the Last Supper. He reclines at Jesus' side when they all eat together. He seems to be the unnamed disciple who follows Jesus after this arrest and goes into the courtyard of the high priest's palace (John 18:15–16). A chapter later, he stands at the foot of the cross with Mary the mother of Jesus, Mary Magdalene, and Jesus' aunt, Mary the wife of Clopas.

Then in chapter 20, the anonymous disciple whom Jesus loves in a special way runs to the tomb ahead of Peter. It is this anonymous disciple who becomes the first person in John's Gospel to believe in Jesus risen from the dead. He enters the empty tomb, sees the burial garments left by the risen Jesus, and leaps to faith. He becomes the only person in any of the Gospels whose Easter faith is not triggered by an appearance of the risen Jesus but simply by the sight of the open and empty tomb.

What makes the anonymous disciple so ready to believe? It is his special love that prompts him into reading positively the ambiguous sign of the empty tomb with its tidy grave clothes and leap to faith. A particular bond of friendship had sprung up between him and Jesus. That loving friendship led to share the Lord's suffering and death. He did not run away like the other male disciples. He took his place at the foot of the cross. He loved Jesus and will take care of the Blessed Virgin Mary. On the first Easter morning, it was his love that led the beloved disciple so easily to a new faith that now included Jesus as risen from the dead.

Some people say, "love is blind." In *Midsummer Night's Dream* and *As You Like It*, several of Shakespeare's characters dismiss love as a "madness" that can lead us away from the real world. John's Gospel shows us that love is not blind. We see with our hearts. It is his heart that let the beloved disciple see the truth of Jesus' resurrection from the dead. We see and truly know what we love, or rather we see and truly know the people whom we love. The beloved disciple loves Jesus, and with the eyes of love truly sees him as gloriously alive.

We all need some of that love, the love that will keep us close to Jesus at all times. Love can keep us there with Jesus: in good times and in bad times, in joy and in sorrow, at happy meals and at grim crucifixions. When love keeps us near Jesus, we will have the eyes to see him in his resurrection and to see his risen power at work in our lives.

Without love we are just voices whispering in the dark. But with love, darkness goes away, light dawns, and faith comes.

With love, we too can see and believe, and keep on believing in Jesus, our risen Lord.

Mere seeing is not always believing. But seeing with love or seeing with our hearts always means believing. May we all see Jesus with our hearts. If we do that, we will always believe in and continually rejoice in our risen Lord.

4

The Real Thomas
(John 20:19–31)

In his classic film *Jesus of Nazareth*, Franco Zeffirelli followed the tradition of picturing St. Thomas as a kind of first-century skeptic, someone who greets surprising news with a shrug of his shoulders. But does this image of "the doubting Thomas" miss something of the picture drawn of Thomas in John's Gospel?

When Jesus appears to the disciples on the evening of the first Easter Sunday, they are hiding away in fear behind locked doors (John 20:19). Where is Thomas? Seemingly he is out bravely showing his face around town. He is not afraid like the others, or at least does not let fear lock him up in hiding.

Earlier in the Gospel, Thomas has already shown himself to be more courageous than the other disciples. When Jesus gets word that his friend Lazarus is seriously ill, he tells the disciples: "Let us go back to Judea." They remind Jesus that Judea and Jerusalem are very dangerous territory; shortly before some hostile critics had tried there to stone Jesus to death. But Thomas will not be put off and bravely says: "Let us go with Jesus so that we may die with him" (John 11:1–16).

That scene portrays a person who can courageously face danger and even death. Yet he is someone who cannot believe in new life, the wonderful new life of the resurrection. Have you met people like Thomas? I have—people who can face up to serious danger and even death itself but find it hard to accept the marvelous news of Jesus' risen life and victory over death.

The lovely thing about Thomas, though, is that when he does meet the risen Jesus, he can come out with the most striking confession of faith in John's Gospel: "My Lord and my God." Thomas looks at the risen Jesus and immediately goes beyond what he sees, Jesus in his risen human body. He now worships him in terms of what he cannot yet see: Jesus in his personal identity as divine Lord.

It is Thomas who pulls together for us the whole of John's Gospel. That Gospel opens with the coming of Christ: "...the Word became flesh and dwelt amongst us. And we looked upon his glory, the glory of the only Son of the Father" (John 1:14). Now at the end of the whole story, Thomas looks upon Jesus risen in glory and worships him. Contemplating first the incarnate Son of God and then contemplating him when risen from the dead establish markers for the beginning and the end of the Gospel according to John.

Let us join Thomas in contemplating the risen Jesus and saying with hearts full of joy and faith, "My Lord and my God."

5
"I Am the Bread of Life"

Every one of us is hungry and constantly searches for life and the fullness of life. Modern advertising knows that we all hunger for life. Contemporary advertisements appeal to that hunger and try to sell us all manner of products.

When I started living in Rome many years ago, I used to improve my Italian by reading the ads on the stations in the city's subway system. What struck me instantly was how often the advertising promised to improve and enhance our lives. One brand of cheese offered to make its customers "live in good form and live better." A huge advertisement for milk guaranteed to help milk drinkers toward "a better life." A particular Riesling wine held out "the pleasures of life." To encourage more people to take part in the annual marathon, the city administration urged Romans to "live sport." A political party ran its campaign with the slogan: "More life, less bureaucracy." It intrigued me whenever I checked advertising in the Roman subway system. All that publicity for food, drink, sport, and political engagement promised clients a richer, more satisfying life.

After I left Rome in 2006 and came to live in London, I found how commercials in the United Kingdom were also in the business of selling us life. When I bought a couple of books in a large Oxford bookstore, the plastic bag I was given carried the message: "Live life. Buy the book." A supermarket made the claim for the food it sold: "Making life taste better." A new brand of motorcar was being promoted as "full of life." A travel agency pushed cheap flights to Asia with the invitation: "Hong Kong. Live it! Love it!" A cell phone urged us: "Improve your social life with free weekend calls." A charming young singer sold her debut album by announcing, "This is the life."

Whatever the value of the particular items being promoted, the messages repeatedly converge on one magic word: *life.* They rely on the fact that we all want to live and live more fully. Commercials constantly promise customers a richer, more satisfying life. Buy this cell phone and "live beyond frontiers," as one ad puts it. Pay for this sports channel and "live the legend" says another advertisement.

Color supplements of weekend papers present us relentlessly with the glittering lifestyles of glamorous celebrities and try to make us desperate to follow them. If we don't, we won't live life on center stage. Commercials tirelessly try to persuade us that there is something missing in our lives. If we buy, consume, and own their products, that will be the way out of our depression. Be a consumer or be nothing.

Advertisers know that we all hunger for a full and worthwhile existence. What we buy, own, and consume will never provide us with the fullness of life, and may well leave us as dissatisfied as ever. In his book *Jesus of Nazareth* Pope Benedict XVI commented on the rich glutton in the parable of Dives and Lazarus: "His carousing was only an attempt to smother the interior emptiness" of his existence. So where is real life to be found? What or who will fill our emptiness and truly satisfy us?

St. John identifies Jesus as "the bread of life," even Life itself. Gloriously risen from the dead, Jesus is *the* source of life, real life here and hereafter. That message of life runs right through John's Gospel. At the end, just in case some readers may have missed the point, John reaches his closing punch line by stating: "These things have been written so that you may come to believe that Jesus is the Messiah, the Son of God, and through believing you might have *life* in his name" (John 20:31).

For us to experience the risen Jesus now, whether in the Eucharist or in so many other ways, is to experience someone who offers to us and delivers to us real life in abundance. He is the fullness of life, Life itself. The promises made by commercials cannot be fulfilled. What we buy and what we own are not going to fill the emptiness of our hearts. Yet commercials have the merit of reminding us vividly that we all yearn for life and want the very fullness of life.

It is from Jesus that we can receive for ourselves and share with others something of the vitality of his risen life. Many of us will have seen that classic film *Jesus of Nazareth*, directed by Franco Zeffirelli. One of its masterful features was the way Zeffirelli brought together for dramatic effect different episodes from the life of Christ. He combined, for instance, the feeding of the five thousand with Mary Magdalene finding Christ—or rather, being found by him. A memorable camera shot picked her out in the crowd. She bit on a hunk of bread before bursting into tears of joy. With her hands tightly grasping the bread and her moist eyes fixed on Jesus, she knew that she had discovered the One who is Life itself. Her hungry heart had found the One who promises: "Whoever comes to me will never hunger." That picture of Mary Magdalene matches perfectly a line from the prize-winning hymn: "You satisfy the hungry heart." Yes, Jesus does satisfy our hearts, fully and forever. When we come to him, we will never hunger.

At every Eucharist, the risen Jesus shows himself to be utterly satisfying and totally fulfilling. He is charged with endless vitality and a spiritual energy that transforms and sustains our existence. Give him half a chance. Let his vital presence in the Eucharist work on you. May we all find in him the bread of life, the bread for our lives now and in the world to come.

Eternal life is what Jesus promises us. It is his to give; he is Life itself in person. In him, with him, and through him, we can truly "live beyond frontiers" and live forever. He is "full of life." Looking at him, we can only say: "This is the life."

6

The Resurrection According to Paul

As the earliest Christian writer or at least the earliest Christian writer whose texts have come down to us, St. Paul opens a window on what the very first Christians believed and practiced. Through his letters we can glimpse what they preached and professed and how they worshiped.

In particular, Paul opens a window on their faith in the resurrection of the crucified Jesus. At the same time, the great apostle makes his own contribution by adding his firsthand witness to the risen Jesus and by interpreting in fresh ways the great truth of the resurrection. To illustrate this double function of Paul, let me take up four distinct themes about the resurrection:

1. The postresurrection appearances of the risen Christ
2. The identity of God as the God of resurrection
3. The link between the Eucharist and the resurrection
4. The cosmic promise conveyed by Christ's resurrection.

First of all, in a letter written around AD 54, Paul quotes a concise formula about the resurrection that he had received when he joined the Christian community around AD 35. He reminds the faithful in Corinth of this common testimony, which went back to the origins of the Christian movement: "I handed on to you as of prime importance what I also received: that Christ *died* for our sins in accordance with the Scriptures, that he was buried, that he *has been raised* on the third day in accordance with the Scriptures, and that he appeared to Cephas [= Peter], then to the Twelve" (1 Cor 15: 3–5 [italics mine]). Two verbs form the heart of this ancient formulation: "died" and "has been raised." The formula centers on Christ's death and resurrection and presents it as supported by historical and biblical evidence. Historically, the burial of Christ establishes the reality of his death: he was truly "dead and buried." The appearances to Peter and then to the core group of Jesus' original disciples ("the Twelve") establish the truth of the resurrection. Further, the death and resurrection took place "in accordance with the scriptures." Those who had deeply pondered the inspired Scriptures they had inherited from Judaism (our Old Testament) should have been predisposed to accept the resurrection of the crucified Jesus. The formula does not cite any particular biblical texts. However, we should think of passages that we know the first Christians treasured, such as the violent death of the servant of the Lord (Isa 52:13—53:12) and the glorious exaltation to God's right hand of "my Lord" (Ps 110:1).

After recalling this key formula that he had received about Christ's resurrection from the dead, Paul presses on in the next verses (1 Cor 15:6–7) to list other appearances of the risen Christ that he knew of. Finally, he adds his own personal testimony: "Last of all, he appeared also to me" (1 Cor 15:8). That meeting with the risen Jesus transformed the way Paul thought about God and about himself. It was *the* moment of grace which the apostle treasured for a lifetime. But what was it like?

In the Book of Acts, Luke describes three times Paul's meeting with Jesus on the road to Damascus (Acts 9, 22, and 26) and has a fair amount to say about that encounter. But Paul himself remains discreet and even laconic. He has few words to say when it comes to reporting his life-transforming experience of the risen Jesus.

We have just cited the brief statement, "he [Christ] appeared also to me." Earlier in the same letter, instead of phrasing matters in terms of the risen Christ "showing himself" or "letting himself be seen," Paul recalls the encounter that made him an apostle: "I have seen the Lord" (1 Cor 9:1). But what was it like to "see" the risen Lord? In another letter the apostle remains equally laconic when he states that God "revealed" his Son "to me" (Gal 1:16). Once again Paul's version of his Damascus road experience does not press beyond a very general expression about the Son being disclosed to him. We are left with the question: What was this revelation of the Son of God like?

In another letter Paul lets us inside his experience of the risen Jesus when he writes: "The God who said 'Let light shine out of darkness' has shone in our hearts to give the light of the knowledge of the glory of God on the face of Jesus Christ" (2 Cor 4:6). When we remember that in the Scriptures "glory" often overlaps with "beauty," we can say that in a new act of creation, which evokes the original creation of light, God let Paul glimpse the divine beauty on the face of Christ. The beautiful Christ took over Paul's existence, became his great love, and transformed his existence forever. After that meeting with the beautiful, risen Lord, Paul was driven by one desire only: to spread everywhere the good news about the crucified and risen Jesus.

Secondly, through Paul's letters, we catch sight of a new way in which the Christian community described God: as the Father who had raised Jesus from the dead (e.g., Gal 1:1; 1 Thess 1:10). Being Jewish, the first Christians had inherited various ways of speaking about God: for instance, as the God of "Abraham, Isaac, and Jacob," as the God who had brought his people out of Egypt, and the rest. In the aftermath of Jesus' resurrection from the dead, they saw God through the lens of the first Easter and added a further divine "attribute." They now spoke of God as the One who had raised and glorified the crucified Jesus.

Paul made his own contribution to this language by stating forcefully that belief in God stands or falls with the resurrection. When some of the Corinthian Christians began to have doubts about the resurrection of Jesus, Paul insisted: '...if Christ has not been raised, then our proclamation has been in vain and your faith has been in vain. We are even found to be *misrepresenting God*' (1 Cor 15:14–15 [italics mine]). Obviously it would be tragic for preachers to proclaim and their audience to believe something that is simply untrue—about what had happened to the dead Jesus and how they should live in the light of that belief. But in religious matters an even greater error would be to "misrepresent" God. To doubt or deny the resurrection means doubting or denying God. In other words, faith in the God who has raised the dead Jesus and will raise us with him is no optional extra for Paul. Easter shapes and colors the very identity of God.

Some Christian groups in Britain have reacted to current publicity for atheism by paying for such countersigns as "There definitely is a God. So start investigating and enjoy eternal life." Paul would want them to be more specific: "There definitely is the God of resurrection. So start investigating and enjoy eternal life."

Thirdly, after he was baptized and joined the Christian community, Paul found believers to be already celebrating the Eucharist on the Lord's Day (Sunday) as their central act of worship. In his turn, he introduced eucharistic practice when he founded local churches in Corinth and elsewhere. In the light of the Eucharist, he found it intolerable that factions split the Corinthian community. When seeking to heal these divisions, he reminded the faithful of what Jesus did at the Last Supper: "On the night he was handed over, the Lord Jesus took bread, and, after giving thanks, he broke it and said: 'This is my body which is for you. Do this in memory of me.' In the same way, he took the cup, after supper, and said: 'This cup is the new covenant in my blood. Whenever you drink it, do this in memory of me'" (1 Cor 11:23–25).

After recalling the words and gestures that Jesus used at the Last Supper, Paul drew out the meaning of the Eucharist for the Christians at Corinth: "...as often as you eat this bread and drink this cup, you proclaim the death of the [risen] Lord until he comes" (1 Cor 11:26). In this way Paul summed up the meaning and message of the Eucharist as preaching the death of Christ, now invisibly but really present in his risen glory, and hoping for his future coming when human history ends. There is a straight line from what Paul wrote to the eucharistic acclamation: "When we eat this bread and drink this cup, we proclaim your death, Lord Jesus, until you come in glory."

Jesus instituted the Eucharist to express through this great sacrament what his death and resurrection would bring: an intimate fellowship among his followers (through a new covenantal relationship with God), which would endure until the final kingdom came. When tackling divisions that plagued the Christian community at Corinth, Paul went to the heart of the matter. By celebrating the Eucharist, they were proclaiming among themselves and to the world the death and resurrection of Jesus their Lord as they waited for his future coming in glory. How then could they tolerate the divisions that were wounding their union in the body of Christ?

Fourthly, when we read Paul's letters attentively, we can spot some development in his thinking about Christ's resurrection and its impact. In his very first letter, Paul reflects on the resurrection within a framework that his fellow Christians shared with him. When witnessing to their hopes about the final coming of Christ in glory, they and Paul think simply of the men and women who make up the Christian community, both those who will be dead and those who will still be alive at the coming of the Lord (1 Thess 4:13–18). All the faithful will be equally blessed at the end, and will live forever with the risen Lord.

Ten years or so later, Paul's own horizon of thought about the resurrection has expanded dramatically. He now understands the resurrection to be working itself out, through the power of the Holy Spirit, for the good of the whole created world. The new age of final freedom from decay and death has already begun, and is a foretaste of the future, transformed universe. Whether they are aware of this or not, all human beings and the entire cosmos are in fact living in expectation of the definitive, glorious transformation that will come (Rom 8: 18–25).

In conclusion, there are four areas in which Paul opens a window for us on the Easter faith of the earliest Christians and what that faith entailed for him personally. Beyond question, there is much more to be added about that Easter faith and Paul's reflections on it. But it is worth exploring at least these four areas. They let us see where the apostle adds precious details about his meeting with the risen Lord and his own insights about what Christ's resurrection involves for the identity of God, the celebration of the Eucharist, and Christian hope for the whole of humanity and the created universe.

From June 2008 to June 2009, Catholics and many other Christians celebrated the Year of St. Paul. It was a lively reminder, especially to pause and reflect on how the great apostle has enriched our knowledge and appreciation of the glorious resurrection of Jesus and what it holds out to us.

7

The Body Language of Love

There are no better crash courses in the body language of love than Italian weddings. During more than thirty years in Rome, invitations to perform the marriage service for Carolina and Stefano and other couples drew me repeatedly into such training courses in love.

When Carolina and Stefano decided to marry, it was obvious that there had been painful wounds in both families. But, as always seems to happen at an Italian wedding, burdens were laid aside, quarrels forgotten, and love transformed everyone— from the grandparents right down to the tiny children of younger relatives. Love shone forth with a smiling, reconciling joy that expressed itself above all in body language. Those who feel an urgent need to be hugged and kissed should get themselves invited to such Italian weddings. Stefano and Carolina led the way, with hugs and kisses that began in the church and flourished at the reception.

The crucifixion and resurrection of Jesus, the events that liberated us from the painful wounds of evil, were nothing if not bodily. The Son of God's love expressed itself above all in the body language of his death upon the cross and his resurrection from the grave. Rising to new life, Jesus reaches out and puts his transforming arms around everyone. The powerful love of the cross draws us together, and his glorious victory over death changes us forever. In his dying and rising, the love of Jesus expressed itself in body language.

Shortly before he died his love manifested itself in the body language of the Eucharist. In that great sacrament he does not shrink from giving himself to us in a very bodily fashion. The body language of the Eucharist draws us together to Jesus and to one another, and transforms our relationship with him and with each other.

Over more than three decades, people at Italian weddings offered me constantly a vivid image of what Jesus wants to do for all of us through his body language. He longs to put his arms around each and all of us and fill us with enduring happiness.

Italian weddings are wonderful experiences, but they last only a few hours. Jesus invites us to his Italian wedding that will never end. He puts his arms around us and offers us a reconciling love that will last for ever and ever.

Part Five

OUR GOD

1

God and the Seasons of Our Lives

The Letter to the Hebrews begins with one of the most majestic opening passages in the entire Bible: "In former times God spoke to our ancestors in a fragmentary and varied fashion through the prophets. But in these last days he has spoken to us by the Son" (Heb 1:1–2). The anonymous writer of Hebrews sums up thus the whole history of God's dealings with the chosen people. God spoke to his people little by little, in ways that were partial and various and yet were constant and faithful—in preparation for the final, definitive word he spoke in and through the Son.

Over the centuries, God spoke gradually and partially in a message that slowly unfolded from Abraham, through Moses, to David, and on to the prophets. Abraham and Sarah were called to leave their native land and become a blessing for "all the families of the earth" (Gen 12:3). Moses was called to bring his brothers and sisters out of captivity and mediate to them a special covenant with God. David was called to be the forefather of the coming Savior.

The prophets also made their contributions. In God's name, some spoke words of comfort and others spoke words of rebuke. Isaiah announced: "Unto us a son is born, unto us a son is given. And the government will be upon his shoulder, and his name will be called Wonderful Counselor, Mighty God, Everlasting Father, Prince of Peace" (Isa 9:6). Through Jeremiah came God's reaction to his people's apostasy: "...my people have forsaken me, the fountain of living water, and dug out cisterns for themselves, cracked cisterns that can hold no water" (Jer 2:13).

There is a point for us in the whole story that Hebrews evokes. God gradually educates us, just as he gradually educated his people. God wants to speak to each of us and reveal what we mean to him and what he wants us to become. However, God does this gradually and not all at once. There are seasons and stages in our lives. The stages may run for six months, a year, three years or seven years. Each stage is a little era for us and each era has its providential message. Like the Israelites, we face times when we suffer in exile and also times when we feel close to God. At times, we are in Egypt or Babylon, at other times in Jerusalem, the city of peace. We have our years of captivity and our years of freedom. All the time we can glimpse God's plan unfolding majestically. His message can assume greater meaning, greater appeal, and greater sternness.

Whatever happens, God speaks to us in various ways; the message is never quite the same. What he said to Moses was more than and different from what he had said to Abraham and Sarah. Likewise each stage of our life brings a new message from God and a new experience of God. We can always be confident that God will speak to us, just as he continued faithfully to speak to his people. A word will come to us, and will come to us with such sweetness and power as to make our answer easy. "The word," St. Paul insists, "is near you; it is on your lips and in your heart" (Rom 10:8).

When we look back on all the seasons and stages of our lives, we can recall words that God has spoken to us—at some point and through some person. We can feel sorrow that our ears have not always been open to catch God's words to us. The complaint that came through Isaiah has not lost its sting: "Why was no one there when I came? Why did no one answer when I called?" (Isa 50:2). Remembering past failures to hear the word of God must put us on the alert for the new things God wishes to say to us now and in the future.

We can be sure of one thing. The God who spoke to our ancestors in "many and diverse ways" will faithfully continue to do the same for each one of us. Let us be all ears to hear the providential message of God at *this* stage and in *this* season of our life.

2
"The Father and I Are One" (John 10:30)

This is one of the most famous statements from the Gospel of John. But what does it mean? Jesus is not saying that he and the Father are a single person, but that they are inseparable. Together they are one God. God is one and unique, and in that one God, Jesus and his Father are utterly united. Jesus includes himself with his Father in the unique identity of the one God.

Within this divine identity, there is a uniquely intimate relationship between the Father and the Son. They need each other to be what they are. The Father is called Father only because Jesus is his Son. Jesus is called "Son" only because he is the Son of his divine Father. Each is essential to the identity of the other.

This is a uniquely intimate relationship. However, it does not swallow up the Son in the Father, or vice versa. Their relationship is the closest that we might ever conceive or imagine. But it is a relationship that differentiates them. Father and Son are utterly inseparable but truly distinct.

This famous statement, "The Father and I are one," carries enormous implications for each of us. We too, in our own way and through the Holy Spirit, enjoy an intimate relationship with Father and Son. We need this one, unique God to be what we are. God is essential to our identity. That is why we worship together each Sunday, because we know that God is utterly essential to our identity. We want to let God, on Sunday and right through the week, develop our intimate relationship with him. That is what the practice of our Christian life is ultimately about: letting the Father and the Son, through the Holy Spirit, bless and enrich our intimate relationship with our God.

It is not that our intimate relationship with God will swallow us up or reduce our personal identity. It is rather the opposite. The closer we come to God, the more we will be ourselves. We are and remain what we are because of our intimate relationship with God. We must give God every chance to let that intimate relationship grow and flourish, even beyond anything we might have imagined for ourselves.

Let us hear Jesus say, "The Father and I are one." And let us pray, "Jesus, help me through the Holy Spirit to grow always in that intimate relationship with you and with the Father, a relationship that is utterly essential to my identity, that relationship that will make me what I am called to be."

3

The God of All Comfort

Several years ago a group of Christians in London invited me to lead a bible study on "the God of all comfort." I knew that the phrase came from the opening chapter of St. Paul's Second Letter to the Corinthians. Before rereading the whole of the epistle, I thought it might be useful to look up the theme on the Internet and then in some English translations of that letter.

An Enduring Image

Upon searching the Internet, the results were astonishing. Typing in "the God of all comfort" brought up nearly one million entries. "The God of all comfort" is certainly alive and well in cyberspace.

Paul would have been pleased at the continuing success of his phrase, "the God of all comfort." It deserves that success; it is a golden thread that Paul allows to run through the Second Letter to the Corinthians. In the first nine chapters, he uses the noun "comfort" and the corresponding verb "to comfort" twenty-five times. His key message is clear: God *comforts* Paul, that is to say, actively strengthens Paul *in* and *in proportion to* his sufferings. The apostle calls those sufferings "affliction," and he refers to his "affliction" ten times in the first nine chapters, and then in chapter 11 tells his readers precisely what form his affliction has taken. Paul insists: "Yes, my sufferings are very real, but God has mightily comforted me in those sufferings."

The Puzzle of Translation

Apropos of translating Paul from his original Greek, it was William Tyndale who, in his 1525 version of the New Testament, rightly chose to render as "comfort" the Greek verb *parakaleō* and noun *paraklēsis* that Paul uses so often in 2 Corinthians. The Douai version of the New Testament in 1582 and the Authorized Version (often called the King James Version) in 1611 followed suit, translating our phrase as "the God of all comfort." In 1952, the Revised Standard Version (RSV) maintained this rendering, and so too did the New International Version (NIV) of 1978.

Many of the other modern translations have, regrettably, dropped "the God of all comfort." In the Revised English Bible (REB 1989), it becomes "the God whose consolation never fails us." Two changes have come in here. "Comfort" has become "consolation"; "all" (which carries a "global" or even spatial feeling with it) picks up connotations of time: "never fails us." At no time will God fail us. The New Revised Standard Version (NRSV 1989) also opts for "consolation" but keeps "all" in translating the phrase: "the God of all consolation." The New Jerusalem Bible (NJB 1985) moves further away, and gives the rendering: "the God who gives every possible encouragement." "Every possible" has replaced "all" and "encouragement" has taken over from "comfort." The New American Bible (NAB, 1970) also goes for "encouragement" but keeps "all" to translate Paul's words as "the God of all encouragement." This picture of God as a very encouraging God weakens, I fear, what Paul wrote and meant, and makes God seem a little like a heavenly teacher or schoolmistress who gives every possible encouragement to the boys and girls in his or her charge.

Today's English Version (TEV, the New Testament portion in 1966), also known as Good News for Modern Man, introduces "help," which also might seem to weaken matters. It translates Paul's phrase as "the God from whom all help comes."

Comfort Ye My People

A further problem with these translations, from the REB to TEV, concerns the Old Testament. A reader of these modern translations could miss the connection between Paul's phrase and the Greek version of the Old Testament, which he and other early Christians knew and used. I am thinking here of the wonderful words at the beginning of Isaiah 40: "Comfort, O comfort my people." These words go back to the sixth century BC. The exile in Babylon is almost over, and God wants to comfort powerfully the suffering people. In his *Messiah*, George Frederick Handel, as we all know, took up those words from Isaiah, and so too did the seventh-century German hymn known from Catherine Winkworth's version, "Comfort, Comfort Ye My People."

When he began his second letter to the Christian people of Corinth with a message of divine comfort, comfort coming in the midst of his and their suffering, Paul may have wanted his readers to recall Isaiah and a similar message of comfort delivered centuries before to a suffering people who were enduring exile and oppression in ancient Babylon. The second part of the Book of Isaiah began just that way in chapter 40, with words of comfort to those who suffer. The Apostle might well have intended to echo that language and message. Even if Paul did not consciously intend the echo, his language and message about "the God of all comfort" does in fact parallel what we read at the beginning of Isaiah 40: "Comfort, O comfort my people."

Curiously, despite dropping "the God of all comfort" in 2 Corinthians, some modern translations, keep the language of "comfort" in Isaiah 40:1. Thus the NRSV, for instance, translates that verse: "Comfort, O comfort my people." The REB also stays in touch with the traditional version: "Comfort my people; bring comfort to them."

The Harsh Reality

It can be interesting, even intriguing, to see how Paul's language in 2 Corinthians has been repeated, translated, and adapted. But the harsh reality of life is more significant, and it touches us critically. After acknowledging "the God of all comfort," the apostle presses on to list some harsh realities of his own ministry. In chapter 6, we read: "...as servants of God we commend ourselves in every way: through great endurance, in afflictions, hardships, calamities, beatings, imprisonments, tumults, labors, watching, hunger...in honor and dishonor, in ill repute and good repute." Then Paul adds some wonderful paradoxes: "We are treated as impostors and yet are true; as unknown and yet well known; as dying and behold we live; as punished and yet never killed; as sorrowful, yet always rejoicing; as poor, yet making many rich; as having nothing, and yet possessing everything" (2 Cor 6: 4–5, 8–10).

Paul uses marvelous language. It may leave us wondering precisely what Paul is referring to here in 2 Corinthians. If that is our question, he answers it a little bit later. In chapter 11 he spells out how he has been imprisoned, beaten, and in other ways close to death: "Five times I have received the forty lashes less one. Three times I have been beaten with rods; once I was stoned. Three times I have been shipwrecked; a night and a day I have been adrift at sea." On his "frequent journeys" he has experienced "danger from rivers, danger from robbers, danger from my own people, danger from Gentiles, danger in the city, danger in the wilderness, danger at sea, danger from false brethren; in toil and hardship, through many a sleepless night, in hunger and thirst, often without food, in cold and exposure. And, apart from these things, there is the daily pressure upon me of my anxiety for all the churches" (2 Cor 11:24–28).

Only a few Christians today could come up with a list of physical and mental sufferings like that. Yet we all have our sufferings and our worries. We too experience "the daily pressure" of our deep anxieties and persistent worries about ourselves, our families, our country, our Church, and our world. Paul's key message then and now remains the same. Our physical and mental afflictions can take all kinds of forms. But in that suffering we can always look to "the God of all comfort," the Father of our Lord Jesus Christ. Our God is the unfailing source of true strength and real comfort.

Paul's Experience

How did Paul know that this message was true? Was he, so to speak, teaching something theoretical, part of the package of Christian faith? Rather he knew the truth of his message through his own personal experience of affliction and comfort. In 2 Corinthians, he also called his afflictions "weakness." He ended the letter by telling his readers in Corinth about his "weakness" as a traveling missionary. When he had found himself in terrible weakness, through the power of God he experienced great strength. In his ministry for the Lord, he had known that paradoxical conjunction of weakness and strength. It was precisely when he was weak that, through God's grace, he found himself to be strong (2 Cor 12:10). Paul may use other terms, but "the God of all comfort" proves the golden thread that runs through the whole letter.

So long live William Tyndale, the Douai New Testament, the Authorised Version, the RSV, the NIV, and the Internet. They all provide the same robust translation of Paul's phrase, "the God of all comfort." God is like that. In and through his terrible sufferings, Paul knew how comforting and consoling it was to worship and obey "the God of all comfort." So too did an exiled and oppressed people in Babylon, to whom the message came in the Book of Isaiah: "Comfort, O comfort my people."

At the Colosseum

My most vivid experience of the truth of Paul's message about the God of all comfort who strengthens us in our afflictions came at the Colosseum in Rome, on May 7, 2000. On a rather damp afternoon Pope John Paul II led an ecumenical commemoration of the innumerable witnesses of faith who had lived and died in the twentieth century. Anglicans, Orthodox, Roman Catholics, and Protestants from various Christian denominations joined the pope in remembering with gratitude and admiration those men and women in all parts of the world who had faced terrible sufferings and often death because of their loyalty to Christ. As well as hymns, scripture readings, and prayers, there were *testimonials* written by or written about these heroes and heroines of faith. Their experiences matched what Paul wrote about himself in 2 Corinthians. These testimonials formed the most striking commentary on Paul's message that I have ever heard or read.

There was a testimony from a Chinese Catholic, Margaret Chou, who was arrested at the age of twenty-two and spent the years from 1958 to 1979 either in prison or in labor camps. She wrote of her experiences: "In the prison factory we worked eighteen hours a day, seven days a week. The drums would wake us up at four in the morning. Before long, due to extreme fatigue, I lost my appetite. At night I collapsed on my bed without even washing my face. The routine kept on for a year. A few days after I arrived at the prison, the officer asked me: 'What is your crime?' I snapped back: 'I did not commit any crime. I was arrested because I was a Catholic and tried to defend my faith.' The officer became very angry and shouted: 'If you did not commit any crime, why are you here?' I was stunned by his extreme anger and shut up. The whole factory was dead silent." Margaret Chou added: "Because of this incident, I discovered several Catholics. We quickly united. Among them was a girl named Tsou. She was especially good to me."

At the Colosseum on that May afternoon, we also heard testimonies about and from witnesses to the faith in Africa and Latin America, as well as from Europe. We heard about people like the German Paul Schneider and the Albanian Anton Luli. Their courageous experience also comments wonderfully on the meaning and truth of St. Paul's message about comfort in affliction and power in weakness.

Comfort of the Afflicted

Paul Schneider, a Lutheran pastor, was born in 1897 and became a member of the anti-Nazi circle founded by Pastor Martin Niemöller. He was arrested and taken to Buchenwald in 1937. In that concentration camp he was the object of mistreatment and torture because he refused to pay homage to Hitler's swastika. In April 1938 he was put into solitary confinement in the camp's bunker, and it was there that he spent the last fourteen months of his life. He died on July 18, 1939, as a result of torture and medical experimentation.

An Austrian priest, who was also imprisoned in Buchenwald but survived, had this to say about Paul Schneider: "In front of the single-storeyed building of the camp, there stretched the immense parade-ground. On feast days, in the silence of the roll-call, suddenly from behind the dark bars of the bunker, there echoed the powerful voice of Pastor Schneider. He would preach like a prophet, or rather he would start to preach. On Easter Sunday, for instance, we heard to our surprise the powerful words: 'Thus says the Lord: "I am the resurrection and the life!"' The long lines of prisoners stood at attention, deeply moved by the courage and energy of that indomitable will. He could never utter more than a few phrases. Then we would hear raining-down blows of the guards' truncheons."

Father Anton Luli, a Jesuit priest, was born in Albania in 1910. Under the Communist regime, he was imprisoned for seventeen years, followed by eleven years of forced labor. Finally, he was released in late 1989, and for the first time could exercise freely his priestly ministry, until he died in 1998. Before his death, he had spoken at an assembly of bishops in Rome. It was this testimony that was read out during the service at the Colosseum in 2000.

"I learned," Luli said, "what freedom is at the age of eighty, when I was able to celebrate my first Mass with the people. The years spent in prison were truly terrible. During my first month, on the night of Christmas, they made me strip and then hung me from the rafters with a rope, so that I could touch the ground only with the tip of my toes. It was cold. I felt the icy chill moving up my body. I was as though I were slowly dying. When the freezing cold was about to arrive at my chest, I let out a desperate cry. My torturers ran to me; they kicked me mercilessly and then took me down. They often tortured me with electricity, putting two electrodes in my ears. It was an indescribably horrible experience. That I remained alive is a miracle of God's grace. I bless the Lord who gave me, his poor and weak minister, the grace to remain faithful to him in a life lived almost entirely in chains. Many of my confreres died as martyrs. It was my lot, however, to remain alive, in order to bear witness."

St. Paul would have treasured these testimonials from Margaret Chou, Anton Luli, and about Paul Schneider. They fill out marvelously St. Paul's message about the Father of mercies who comforts and strengthens us in all our afflictions. That message about "the God of all comfort" remains alive and well nearly two thousand years later.

4

God the Heavenly Chef

In 1987, the Academy Award for the best foreign film went to a film from Denmark entitled *Babette's Feast*. Set in the nineteenth century, it begins by picturing rigidly controlled life in a small village on an island off the Danish coast.

One day a woman arrives from Paris. For political reasons she has fled her own country and takes refuge in this isolated village. What the local people do not know is that Babette is a world-class chef. She lives among them for a time before something unexpected happens.

She wins a major lottery, and decides to spend the money by putting on a big feast for all the people of the village. The film shows a massive quantity of food being brought ashore for the feast: ducks, geese, fish, fruit, pudding, wine, and all kinds of goodies. Babette herself prepares this lavish feast with all the skill and gusto of a leading chef.

The scene can bring to mind a parable in which Jesus imagines something like that (Luke 14:15–24). A landowner who is well off decides to put on a really big dinner. He generously invites a large number of people from the neighborhood to come and enjoy themselves. The landowner gets in lots of fish, roast beef, veal, olives, grapes, red and white wine, and other ancient goodies. As soon as everything is ready, he sends out a servant to let those who have been invited know that the big feast is now waiting for them. The food and drink are about to go on the table.

But those guests who have previously accepted the invitation now decide not to come after all. They begin to make excuses, polite excuses. One says that he has bought an estate and must go out and inspect it. What else would you do if you have just put your money down on some property? Another of those invited has bought a team of oxen, and he wants to try them out, right here and now, instead of attending the big dinner. A third person reports that he has just got married, and, of course, he cannot come. He wants to spend time with his bride, instead of bringing her to the banquet.

They all make excuses: polite, reasonable excuses. For various reasons none of them now, after first saying yes, want to turn up at the delicious dinner and really enjoy themselves. It is all very odd, and it makes the landowner angry. He turns around and invites a whole crowd of other people.

In the parable that Jesus tells, we are obviously meant to think of God, our God who wants to enjoy the company of all of us at his heavenly banquet. This is not just a great party that a top-class chef, like Babette, can put on and pay for herself. What God has in mind for us is the party to end all parties, a party that will never, never end. When God invites us, we must never make excuses, like the people in the parable. An invitation coming from God is always for our good, our total good and our lasting good. We are out of our minds if we turn God down or if we say "yes" and later back out of the invitation.

Let us follow the folk in that little Danish village who accept the invitation from Babette. They come and find themselves enjoying a wonderful feast that goes beyond anything that they have ever eaten or even imagined. God is not just a top-class chef, but is the heavenly chef to end all chefs.

We are out of our minds if we allow any reasons to get in the way of our saying yes to God. We must say yes to God: "Yes, I am coming to your feast. I want to enjoy myself with you, for ever and ever."

Epilogue

The first chapter of this book presented six images that can help us engage in prayer and do so on a regular basis. Let me conclude by adding a seventh image, "rumination." Besides helping some readers settle into prayer, it could also describe what they have all been doing by "pausing for thought" right through this book.

When I grew up on a farm, one of the chores was milking the cows twice daily—before leaving for school and after returning from school. During the milking session the cows consumed some hay and cereals and then returned to the fields to eat whatever grass was available. At certain times during the day they would lie down and "ruminate" or "chew the cud." Rumination involved food returning from their stomach to be chewed a second time before being properly digested.

When I saw the cows chewing the cud on our farm, they often impressed me with their peaceful concentration. They had to chew their food a second time, but they happily applied themselves to the task. Occasionally they flicked their tails to drive flies away. But the dominant mood on their faces was that of quiet, tranquil attention.

A pause for thought, whether it takes the form of spiritual reading or moves on to straightforward prayer, is a kind of peaceful ruminating. If we quietly place ourselves in the presence of God, we may need occasionally to flick away distractions. As long as we take some spiritual food into our heart and peacefully chew the cud, God will surely do the rest for us.

Index of Names

Also by Gerald O'Collins, SJ
Published by Paulist Press

A Concise Dictionary of Theology
(Revised and Expanded Edition)

Easter Faith
Believing in the Risen Jesus

Following the Way
Jesus, Our Spiritual Director

Living Vatican II
The 21st Council for the 21st Century

Pope John Paul II
A Reader
co-edited with Daniel Kendall, SJ, and Jeffrey LaBelle, SJ

Reflections for Busy People
Making Time for Ourselves, Jesus, and God

The Lord's Prayer

The Tripersonal God

green press INITIATIVE

Paulist Press is committed to preserving ancient forests and natural resources. We elected to print this title on 30% post consumer recycled paper, processed chlorine free. As a result, for this printing, we have saved:

3 Trees (40' tall and 6-8" diameter)
1 Million BTUs of Total Energy
303 Pounds of Greenhouse Gases
1,459 Gallons of Wastewater
89 Pounds of Solid Waste

Paulist Press made this paper choice because our printer, Thomson-Shore, Inc., is a member of Green Press Initiative, a nonprofit program dedicated to supporting authors, publishers, and suppliers in their efforts to reduce their use of fiber obtained from endangered forests.

For more information, visit www.greenpressinitiative.org

Environmental impact estimates were made using the Environmental Defense Paper Calculator. For more information visit: www.papercalculator.org.